The Great Deeds of
SUPERHEROES

Published by
PETER BEDRICK BOOKS
2112 Broadway
New York, NY 10023

Published by agreement with Millenium Books, Australia

Library of Congress Cataloging-in-Publication Data
Saxby H.M. (Henry Maurice)
The great deeds of superheroes / retold by Maurice Saxby;
illustrated by Robert Ingpen. —1st American ed.

Includes bibliographical references (p.).
Includes index.
Summary: A collection of tales relating the deeds of heroic
figures through the ages such as King Arthur, Roland, Cuchulain,
Samson, and Jason.
ISBN 0-87226-342-8; 0-87226-260-X (pbk)
1. Heroes—Juvenile literature. (1. Heroes.) I. Ingpen, Robert
R., ill II. Title.
PN56.5.H45S29 1990
808.8'0352—dc20   *90-856*

Printed and bound in Hong Kong

2 4 6 8 9 7 5 3

This edition printed 1993

The Great Deeds of
SUPERHEROES

Retold by Maurice Saxby

Illustrated by Robert Ingpen

PETER BEDRICK BOOKS

NEW YORK

CONTENTS

We all need heroes

"I swear by the oath of my people," said Cuchulain,
"I will make my doings be spoken among
the great deeds of heroes in their strength."

The stories in this book are among the oldest, most exciting and most power-ful in the world. They began so long ago that no one now knows exactly how they came into being. They were first told orally and passed down by word of mouth before being written down on stone, clay, parchment or paper made from papyrus.

Whether or not the heroes of these tales existed and to what extent the details of their lives as we now have them are true we cannot be sure. Probably most of the stories are based on historical fact but, like all legends, they have grown and developed during the centuries of their telling and retelling. What we do know is that the spirit of these wonder tales is true and that they are as meaningful and relevant today as they ever were — perhaps even more so. They remind us of the need for physical and moral strength as well as intelligence and ingenuity in a world that is often cruel, hostile and corrupt. These ancient heroes will always be remembered and admired for their courage and resourcefulness.

The central characters in this collection are all men who represent the active — even aggressive — side of all successful people. They are adventurers; that is they ad-venture, leave home, and go out into the world. This means encountering and overcoming all kinds of obstacles. The stories of female heroines are just as thrilling and inspiring. These deserve a book of their own and will be told in a companion volume.

Each age and culture produces its own representative heroes who, if they are great enough and grand enough, become immortalised in legend. Often they are superhuman — part man part god, because human beings must have idealised heroes to worship. Less often they are folk heroes, humble men and women who represent the common person made a little larger than life — an inch or so taller, somewhat bolder, and a great deal more daring than you or me.

The Heroic Example

The superhuman heroic tradition is universal and enduring—for many reasons. In everyday life we all need leaders or stars to act as models, to admire and copy, to encourage and inspire us to greater achievements. Throughout the ages people have searched for the expression of a supreme being as god. The Hebrews of the Old Testament of the Bible found one God only, Yahweh. The Greeks and the Romans, along with most other cultures, had many gods, although the Greek god Zeus was the ruler of the lesser gods. Most cultures refer to a hierarchy of divine creatures or gods that they worship and supplicate. Filling the gap between the gods and the people are the superheroes of myth and legend. In them we create god-like creatures out of our dreams and ambitions. We see ourselves enlarged— a vision of what we could be were we not limited by our weaknesses. Because our mythical heroes are both human and superhuman, they provide us with an ideal that is within our grasp, not completely impossible and unrealistic.

In our imperfect society, with its increasing demands to achieve success in our study, sport or work, we need to be reassured by stories of a world where all things are possible if we are brave enough, strong and wise enough. We need inner strength to deal with the problems of being human and we need shining examples in our search for the meaning and value of life and for our moral development.

Before the great superheroes there were always stories of the gods. The gods, even when they visited earth in disguise and interfered in the lives of humans, were forever remote. They belonged to Olympus or some other heavenly dwelling place and their power was unattainable. But the sons of the gods were heroic, within our understanding. The great heroes represent the heights of human attainment yet remind us that men are mortal, frail and fallible. The hero who sets out in search of immortality is always disappointed; many a hero is brought low at life's end through an act of betrayal or because he has to pay the price of his own weakness or pride.

The Heroic Pattern

Although each hero is typical of his time in history and his culture there are, in these stories, recurring themes and patterns of behaviour which belong to all ages of history and all cultures. These stories are timeless, multicultural and have a universal appeal, because they are really about the human race opposing the forces of evil in the shape of giants, ferocious animals or superhuman monsters. That is why they sometimes seem violent. Evil stirs up violence. The hero, representative man, succeeds because of his prodigious strength, his intelligence and cunning, his perseverance, his courage, his idealism and, often, with help from the gods or the immortals.

HERO	WEAPON OR TALISMAN	CIRCUMSTANCES OF BIRTH	PROPHECY	TUTOR MENTOR	INFANCY	BOYHOOD AND YOUTH
PERSEUS	Shield of Athena Sandals of Hermes Sickle of Cronos	Fathered by Zeus of Danae, a royal virgin	Oracle foretold that he would kill his grandfather, Acrisius	Hermes Athena	Reared at the court of King of Seriphos	Learnt skills of hunting, fishing, swordsmanship. Overcame monsters
HERACLES	Olive wood club Lion-skin cloak Sword of Hermes	Born of Alcmena and Amphitryon but reputed to be the son of Zeus who assumed the guise of Amphitryon.	Oracle at Delphi told him of his divine origin and commanded him to serve Eurystheus for twelve years	Eurytus, grandson of Apollo and many others	Killed two serpents with his bare hands	At eighteen killed the lion of Mount Cithaeron with a club
THESEUS	Father's sword and sandals	Son of Aegeus of Athens and Aethra, daughter of King of Troezen. His father left his mother before Theseus was born	Aegeus told Aethra to send his son to Athens when he recovers the sword and sandals hidden by Aegeus	Grand-father & mother, also Heracles	Early mastered the manly pursuits	Grew in skill and strength
JASON		Son of Aeson, King of Greek colony of Iolcus in Thessaly	Step-uncle, Pelias, had been warned by oracle to beware of someone wearing only one sandal. Jason fulfilled the prophecy	Centaur Chiron reared him. Hera favour-ed him	Trained as a Hero-Prince	
ODYSSEUS		Son of Laertes, King of Ithaca	The blind prophet Tiresius foretold events of his life	Athena	Unknown	Royal Prince — one of Helen's suitors
GILGAMESH		Son of the goddess Ninsun and a priest of Kullah, from whom he inherits mortality	Subject to dreams	Goddess Ishtar Shamash the sun god	Unknown	Renowned for feats of strength & for restlessness
SIGURD	The sword, Branstock Horse, Greyfell	Fathered by Hiordis and Sigmund, the Volsung	Becomes involved with the curse of the ring	Odin Regin	Reared by mother and stepfather in Denmark	Apprenticed to Regin the dwarf
VAINAMOINEN	Zither	Thirty years in the womb. Son of Earth Mother			Born old	
MOSES	Staff	Born of common folk but claimed by Pharoah's daughter	God speaks to him in the burning bush	Yahweh	Reared at Egyptian court	Attributes of an Egyptian prince
SAMSON	The jawbone of an ass	Common parents but angel appears to mother before birth	Angel promises that he will free his people from Philistines	Yahweh	Strong even as an infant	Kills lion with his bare hands
BEOWULF	Sword	Nephew of King Hygelac			Raised as page	Kills sea monster when swimming in open sea with Breca
ARTHUR	The sword, Excalibur	Born of Igraine, wife of Duke of Tintagel, but fathered by King Uther Pendragon	Merlin promises that his name will be known throughout the land	Merlin Sir Ector	Reared as a prince by Sir Ector	Squire to Sir Kay
CUCHULAIN		Fathered by the god of the Otherworld who appeared to Dechtire of the royal house of Ulster as a mayfly	Cathbad foretold a great name but a short life span	The wise men of Ulster. Cathbad the Druid	Fights with older boys & defeats them	Slays the great hound of Culain
ROLAND	The sword, Durendal Magic horn, Olifant	Nephew of Charlemagne				Fights with Oliver, then claims his friendship
EL CID	The sword, Tizone His horse, Babieca	A noble father, Diego de Vivar	Promise of St. Lazarus that he would be unconquerable	Father		Aids a struggling stranger mindless of danger

INITIATION	TASKS & TRIALS	JOURNEY	STRENGTHS	WEAKNESSES	DEATH
At court of Polydectes	To collect the head of Medusa, the Gorgon	To the Graeae, the land of the Gorgons, Africa	Fearless, decisive	Slew his grandfather, Acrisius, as decreed at birth	Set among the stars after being killed in battle
Consciously chooses virtue to vice & folly	Twelve labours set by Eurystheus	To carry out his labours	Physical strength and daring	Temper and madness sent by Hera	Killed by a poisoned robe. Made immortal and married the goddess Hebe
At eighteen he recovers his father's sword and sandals	A series of tasks on his way to Athens. To slay the Minotaur	To Athens. To Crete with the Argonauts	Grace and strength of will	Despondency. Failure to hoist sail	Murdered by Lycomedes
Ferries Hera, in disguise as an old woman, across a stream. She promises him fame	Sent by Pelias to search for the Golden Fleece. Aeëtes, owner of the Fleece, sets him tasks also	Chief of the Argonauts. Across the Mediterranean & home via Crete	Quick witted & decisive	Accomplice in treachery of his wife Medea, the witch	Killed when part of the *Argo* fell on him from the Temple of Poseidon
	To fight against the Trojans	To Troy and long journey (odyssey) home	Cunning and resourceful. Daring & bold	Offends Poseidon	An easy old age and a gentle death
His wrestling against Enkidu	To slay the monster Humbaba. Quest for everlasting life	In the forest and to Utnashapishtim, the Faraway	Courage, strength and vision. Friendship	Restlessness of spirit	Died, but his name lives on engraved in stone
Draws the sword of Odin from the oak tree, Branstock	The slaying of Fafnir	To Hindfell and the awakening of Brynhild	Handsome, noble of mind and body	Ignores curse and bewitched by Grimhild	Murdered by stab wounds. Brynhild joins him on funeral pyre. Goes to Valhalla
	To find the lost words. Life was a series of labours	To Pohja and the Kingdom of the Dead	Singer, craftsman. Determination	Looks upward when forbidden	Sang into being a magic boat which bore him into the sky. Promised to come again
Kills Egyptian and aligns himself with the Hebrew people	Freeing the children of Israel from yoke of Pharoah	Exodus and journey through the wilderness	A resolute leader. A law giver	Disobeys God	Buried in the land of Moab—Grave unknown. Mourned for thirty days
Sets foxes loose in cornfields of Philistines	To free Israelites from Philistines		Physical strength	Succumbs to a Philistine woman. Betrayed	Dies with his enemies in collapse of temple court
Night battle in the deeps	The slaying of Grendel and Grendel's mother	To Denmark	Strongest man alive—fearless & bold		Slain in battle with monster. Hero's monument erected over treasure-trove
Draws sword from the stone	Those of knighthood and chivalry	Against Saxon invaders	Courteous, brave and just. Sets up Round Table	Too trusting	Slain in battle at Camlann. Sleeps in Avalon until the hour of greatest need
Takes up arms and slays the three sons of Nechtar	To win the Champion's Portion		The bravest of all	Blood-lust	Beheaded in battle, but hero-light shone like a halo. Emer, his wife, joins him in a common grave
	To fight for his uncle, the Emperor	To Roncesvalles	Steadfast friendship	Pride	Died in battle undefeated. His soul received by St. Gabriel in Paradise
Defends his father's honour and fights the Count of Lozano. Dubbed Knight of Castile	To fight the Moors and bring honour to Castile	Expeditions through Spain	Generosity of spirit. Bold daring		Falls in combat but his embalmed body is laced to the saddle of his horse and he appears as a vision to his enemies

But even though one monster is slain there is often another to take its place. The battle between good and evil, right and might, the noble and the ignoble never really ends. The hero must continue in battle until he dies. Then new heroes will be chosen to carry on the fight and sometimes there will be the promise that, as in the story of King Arthur, the hero will sleep until he is raised again at the hour of his country's greatest need. The human race is encouraged by the hope of new heroes for every age or the promise of the return of the god-like heroes of the past.

The Birth of the Hero

Very often the hero is begotten by supernatural means. Zeus comes to Danae in a shower of gold and Perseus is conceived; Zeus visits Alcmena in the form of her husband, Amphitryon, and Heracles is conceived; Lugh of the Long Arm, god of the Otherworld, takes on the form of a mayfly and when Dechtire swallows the mayfly with her wine, Cuchulain is conceived. The mother of Samson was barren until an angel appeared and promised her a child saying, "Behold, you shall conceive and bear a son; so then drink no wine or strong drink, and eat nothing unclean, for the boy shall be a Nazirite to God from birth to the day of his death."

The hero is usually of royal or noble parentage or, like Moses, is adopted by royalty. Sometimes he is threatened at birth like Jason, Arthur and Moses were, and is brought up away from his home; but he is watched over by a superhuman like Chiron, the centaur, or Merlin, the wizard, or, in the case of Moses, by Yahweh (God) Himself. Nearly always we know that the hero is destined to accomplish great deeds.

Boyhood

Often we are told little or nothing of the very early life of the hero, except that we do know that Heracles proved his strength by strangling two huge serpents while he was still in the cradle. Sometimes, as with Jason, he is trained for the life of a hero-prince. Often we learn that the hero acquires with unusual speed the skills and accomplishments that will make him great.

Initiation

Nearly always in his youth or adolescence the hero proves his manhood in some way: killing a wild animal with his bare hands, standing up for a principle or fulfilling some prophetic sign, as when Arthur pulls the sword from the stone.

Task or Quest

Either as part of his initiation, or often because he proves himself at initiation, the hero is given labours to perform, a task to accomplish or a quest to fulfil — hence the labours of Heracles, the golden fleece of Jason's search, the tasks of Perseus set by Polydectes, Sigurd's slaying of Fafnir, Vainamoinen's search for the lost words, Moses's leading the children of Israel out of Egypt to the Promised Land, El Cid's campaign against the Moors and Roland's against the Saracens. Always the hero has the task of fighting against evil or oppression.

The Journey

Almost always the task or quest involves a journey. The journeys of Odysseus and Moses took up to forty years. Many heroes, like Jonah from the Old Testament of the Bible (his story is not told here), made epic journeys just as many modern heroes such as Scott, Amundsen or Hillary who are celebrated for their courageous expeditions.

The Talisman, Sword or Magic Object

Many a hero of old took with him on his journey and into battle a special sword. Perseus was loaned the sickle of Cronos; Sigurd's sword was specially forged by Regin from the preserved shards of his father's weapon; King Arthur had his Excalibur, Roland his Durendal and El Cid his Tizone. Other heroes had objects of power such as Moses's staff, or were from time to time loaned objects by the gods, as when Perseus was equipped for his onslaught against the Medusa.

Feats

Many are the contests and battles recorded among the exploits of the heroes. There are magical contests — Moses against Pharoah, Cuchulain against Curoi. There are single combats against kings, giants, dragons and especially wild animals. The battle is never against ordinary men or animals; the opponent of the hero is always extraordinary. Sometimes the hero has to answer a riddle and always, as with Odysseus, his cunning is as important as his strength and bravery.

Marriage

The hero usually marries but his wife does not accompany him into battle. Even Moses's wife seems relatively unimportant once he enters upon his God-given task. Penelope, the wife of Odysseus, is unusual in that she is waiting for the hero when he returns from his long journeys; the couple are reunited after Odysseus's many adventures.

However, the heroes are not friendless. The name of Gilgamesh will always be linked with that of Enkidu, Roland's with Oliver. Sir Bedivere is with Arthur at the very end.

The Greek heroes sometimes found love through their exploits, as Perseus found Andromeda and Theseus his Ariadne. The story of Sigurd and Brynhild is among the world's great tragedies of love.

Reward and Death

In almost every instance the ancient hero gains the reward of his labours. It is significant that of the two Old Testament heroes in this collection, Samson's reward is achieved by his death and Moses was allowed to see but not to enter the Promised Land.

Yet few of the heroes live on into a peaceful old age. Jason had to face exile; Perseus killed his grandfather by mistake and Theseus inadvertently brought about the death of his father.

The deaths of the Greek Heracles and the Celtic Cuchulain are deeply moving in their tragic proportions. Both took their loved-one to the grave with them. The funeral pyre of Heracles and Cuchulain's cairn are symbolic of their glorious lives. The funeral fire that consumed the body of Heracles and the hero-light which shone like a halo around the shoulders of the dead Cuchulain are lights from the past which have provided a "gleam" for centuries and which still shine for today's readers.

Reliving the lives of these super heroes of the past is an exciting, mind-enlarging and deeply moving emotional experience which gives a new and proper perspective to the rock stars, the cinema heroes and the super-men and women of today. There is a colour, richness, and opulence of detail about the lives of these old heroes that makes today's megastars appear to be clothed in tinsel. Always there is a feeling of fate or destiny and a pattern of life, but never is this mechanical. The gods might intervene, but ultimately it is the hero himself who fulfils his destiny.

Every generation owes a debt to the past—even to its mistakes. If we forget the past we are bound to repeat its mistakes. These hero-tales of ancient civilisations and a glorious past are wonderful stories which have set the pattern for all succeeding epics down through the ages and for the adventure stories of today. The characteristics of the hero may vary over the years and from society to society, but the need for great heroes remains with us constantly. The stories in this present volume of great hero-tales are among the most action-packed, the most dramatic, the most overwhelming and the most awe-inspiring that the world has ever produced.

Ancient Greece

Apart from the Old Testament of the Bible, the most famous stories from ancient times come to us from the Greeks. Ancient Greece was not one country but was made up of many city-states, each of which had its own king and ruling family as well as its own myths and legendary stories.

Because many of the city-states were separated by high mountains communication between them was difficult, so stories varied from place to place. For a long time the stories were passed on by word of mouth, each storyteller relating his own version. Gradually one particular version of a story was accepted by one part of the country while another version of the same story was told in another part of the country. Eventually these different stories were collected and written down, therefore accounting for the many variations of each story that we have today.

The most ancient stories were of the Greek deities — the gods and goddesses. These myths, as they are called, comprise an important part of the religion of ancient Greece. The Greeks had many gods and goddesses, each associated with the essential forces of nature or the great human passions. Poseidon was the god of the sea, Hades the god of the Underworld and Ares the god of war. Aphrodite was the goddess of love, Athena the goddess of wisdom and Demeter the goddess of the harvests, grain and all living plants. Zeus was the king of the gods and Hera was his wife. The gods, or the Immortals, including the many lesser gods, lived on Mount Olympus, thought to be the highest mountain in the world, where they feasted, revelled and sang to the music of Apollo, led by the nine Muses.

From time to time one or more of the gods, including Zeus himself, would visit the earth and play some part in the lives of men and women, sometimes helping them, sometimes punishing them, or even playing pranks; but nothing could happen in the world unless it was allowed by Destiny who maintained order in the universe, even among the Immortals themselves. Destiny revealed all things to Zeus and in turn Zeus spoke to the Greek people either through his own voice or through the oracle of Apollo at Delphi. The winged Hermes with his quick wit and practical jokes was the messenger of the gods and also the god of the herds and of business, with a special interest in thieves.

Sometimes one of the gods, especially Zeus, coupled with a human. Their offspring was a demi-god: part god, part human. So between the gods and mankind the Greeks recognised the hero who was greater than ordinary mortals because of his birth, his superhuman courage, his strength and cleverness. An ancient Greek writer called Hesiod, who lived about 700 B.C., defined a hero as a person who was a kind of link between the gods and ordinary mortals. Heroes represented the ideals of Greek life and society; their exploits and mighty deeds were sung about and held up as examples to look up to, as patterns of behaviour. These heroes provided their society with a sense of pride and a set of values.

After the fall of the great city of Troy, between 600 and 700 B.C., Hesiod, Homer, Pindar and other Greek writers collected and wrote down the myths of the gods and the legendary stories of the heroes. Apollonius of Rhodes (about 250 B.C.) and Apollodorus (about A.D. 100) also gave us versions of the stories. These are the sources of the many modern retellings meant for younger readers, including Nathaniel Hawthorne's *Tanglewood Tales* (1853), Charles Kingsley's *The Heroes* (1856), Andrew Lang's *Tales of Troy and Greece* (1907) and Roger Lancelyn Green's *Heroes of Greece and Troy* (1960).

For a long time modern scholars thought that the old stories were pure imagination but it is now believed that there is probably some faint element of truth in the hero tales. In the nineteenth century a German archaeologist, Heinrich Schliemann, followed Homer's story and unearthed the foundations of Troy and Mycenae.

Even so, the stories are almost entirely poetic for even when they were first written down after long years of oral telling, each poet selected from the many versions those details which stirred his own imagination. So the stories in this book have more than one source and exist in more than one version.

WHAT FOLLOWS IS THE ESSENCE OF A NUMBER OF FAMOUS HERO TALES. TOGETHER THEY GIVE A PICTURE OF WHAT SCHOLARS CALL THE ARCHETYPAL GREEK HERO. EVEN TODAY THE HEROES OF BOOK AND SCREEN ARE DESCENDED FROM THESE ARCHETYPES.

Perseus the Fearless

The ancient land of Argolis was a kingdom of old Greece where stood the cities of Tiryns, Argos and Mycenae, each built by mortals with the aid of the one-eyed Cyclopes, giant servants to Zeus. The king of Argolia was Acrisius of Tiryns, whose wife gave birth to a baby girl whom they called Danae. Overjoyed, the King consulted the oracle to see what the future would hold for her. Instead of good news the oracle prophesied that the child would grow to womanhood and bear a son who would kill his grandfather, Acrisius himself.

To prevent the prophecy from coming true Acrisius shut up his daughter in a tall tower of brass which he kept guarded day and night so that Danae could see no man, let alone marry. Although rumours of Danae's beauty spread afar she remained hidden from any mortal eye.

But not to Zeus who looked with favour on the lovely girl and one night came to her in a shower of gold. He spoke to her and loved her by moonlight. In time they had a child whom Danae called Perseus.

Angrily Acrisius summoned his daughter and demanded to know who it was that had penetrated the tower and secretly wed her. In vain did she try to convince him that it was Zeus himself who had fathered the child.

But in spite of his fear and anger the King could not bring himself to destroy his daughter and his grandson outright. Instead he ordered that they be taken to the seaside and set adrift on the bay of Nauplia in a large wooden chest with neither food nor water. Throughout the night the cradle-chest floated on the sea while Danae prayed to Zeus to protect their helpless baby. In the morning the chest was washed up on the shores of the island of Seriphos, which was ruled by King Polydectes.

The King's brother, called Dictys, often fished in the sea. It was he who discovered the stranded crate with its human cargo. Overcome by Danae's beauty he took her and the child home and cared for them.

Perseus grew up at court—fair to look upon, strong and impressive in his ability to hunt and fish, and excelling at games and in the use of the sword.

As time went by, Polydectes fell in love with Danae and begged her to marry him; but he was a cruel man and Perseus would have none of him. So Polydectes grew to hate Perseus and constantly thought of ways to destroy him . . .

Perseus and the Medusa

One day as Polydectes watched Perseus and his mother strolling together through the palace gardens he snapped his fingers in triumph, for a cunning plan had developed in his mind. He summoned Perseus immediately into his presence.

"I hear that you are too much in the company of your mother and the womenfolk. What manner of man are you? I shall give a feast and invite the strongest and bravest young men in the kingdom and we shall see how your strength measures against theirs."

Perseus knew that what the King implied about his nature was untrue and he seethed inwardly with anger, for he was as strong, brave and daring as any youth in the kingdom.

When the young men arrived for the feast they each brought a valuable gift for the King, but Perseus because of his unfavoured position had nothing. This was what Polydectes had anticipated.

"Didn't I say that you lacked manhood!" he scoffed. And he laughed, as did the other youths, so that Perseus burned inwardly with shame.

"I shall go and win a present finer than any of you have brought!" he shouted.

"Then bring me the head of the Medusa," replied the wily Polydectes, believing that this was the way to rid himself of Perseus and so break down Danae's resistance to him.

"That I shall do," Perseus affirmed, "unless I die in the attempt."

Inwardly Perseus felt less sure of himself than his daring offer implied, for the Medusa was the ugliest and the most terrifying of the Gorgons, monster-creatures who lived in the land of the Hyperboreans. The Medusa had sharp curving talons and each strand of hair was a long, writhing, hissing snake. So terrible was this creature that whoever looked at its face was immediately turned to stone.

Meanwhile Zeus, the father of Perseus, watched from Mount Olympus and was proud of his son's strength and beauty. So he commanded the other Immortals to give Perseus whatever help was in their power. Hermes the messenger-god, bringer of good fortune, presented Perseus with wings for his sandals so that he could move swiftly through space, and said, "I lend you for your task the sickle with which Cronos wounded the sky. Only its blade is sharp enough to sever the head of the Medusa."

It was his companion Athena, goddess of wisdom, her helmet glinting in the sunlight, who spoke next: "I lend you my shield. Use its polished surface as a mirror when you confront the Gorgon. Do not look at the creature's face lest you be turned to stone."

Hermes then stepped forward again. "Now go to the Grey Sisters and they will tell you how to reach the nymphs who live at the back of the North Wind. They will tell you where to find the Gorgon and lend you whatever else you have need of."

So Perseus set off on his quest, his winged sandals bearing him northward over land and sea and along the rim of the sky until he came to a lonely cavern in the frozen wastes of ice and snow — a land of perpetual night. There the daughters of the Titan Phorcys, the Graeae — the Grey Sisters, so called because they were born old and grey and had only one eye and one tooth between them — sat silently passing their one eye from one to the other. They muttered curses upon all who passed through this barren land. Stealthily Perseus crept upon them and as one of them held out the eye to her companion Perseus slipped his hand into hers and grasped the eye.

"Now old women, I have your eye," called Perseus. "Tell me where to find the nymphs who live at the back of the North Wind and I will give it back to you."

"Go to Atlas who holds the heavens on his shoulders. It is his daughters, the Hesperides, who will give you what you want. Now let us have our eye back."

So Perseus returned the eye and winged southward to Mount Atlas and looked down on the garden of the Hesperides who guarded the golden apples of Hera.

"Tell me, fair maidens, how to reach the land of the Gorgons and what I need to kill the Medusa, for I am bound to carry the Medusa's head to Polydectes, the unjust King."

"You already have the sandals of swiftness, the sickle of Cronos and the shield of Athena. All you need is a helmet to make you invisible. There is a cap of dog-skin which belongs to Hades, the god of the Underworld. One of us will fetch it for you." Then one of the nymphs departed swiftly to the kingdom of Hades and returned with the helmet of invisibility.

"Our father Atlas will point you to the island of the Gorgons," they said, "but take one more thing. Here is a wallet in which to carry Medusa's head, for even when it is severed from her body it retains its power to turn men to stone."

So Perseus pulled the helmet over his head and sped to the island littered with the stony statues of travellers and warriors. As he approached he heard the hissing of serpents. Holding Athena's shield above him he looked into its mirrored surface and saw the three loathsome Gorgons below sleeping in the sunlight with the Medusa's head of vipers writhing and spitting venom even while she slept.

Holding the shield of Athena in one hand and the sickle of Cronos in the other, Perseus fell like an arrow on the Medusa. With one sweep of the blade he severed the hideous head and plunged it into the wallet given to him by the nymphs. But even as he did so the other Gorgons awoke, their wings beating the air. They sprang toward Perseus with blood-curdling yells and flew at him, determined to avenge their sister.

Never before had Hermes's sandals been put to better use. Over oceans and continents they bore Perseus until the dreadful sisters were outdistanced. Westward over Africa Perseus flew, bearing his terrible cargo. Even as he flew, drops of Medusa's blood seeped through the wallet and fell on the desert below. At each drop began an oasis on that spot in the desert.

A night passed and when morning came he looked seaward and saw below him what seemed to be a statue carved in stone. Flying closer he saw that it was no statue, but the figure of a beautiful dark-haired girl, naked except for a necklace of precious stone, and that the girl was chained to a rock by her hands and feet. Perseus landed lightly beside her, his heart moved with pity.

"Tell me, poor maiden, who you are and why you are chained here," he called.

"Who speaks out of the wind? I hear a voice but see not even a shadow," the captive girl replied.

Then Perseus removed the helmet of Hades which he wore and materialised fair and god-like from the sea-spray, his image pierced by the sunlight that blew in in drifts from the amethyst of the sea. The sunlight shimmered across the girl's nakedness, clothing her in all its brilliance. "My name is Perseus," he said, and with four quick, powerful blows by the sickle of Cronos he severed the chains which bound the girl. "Now tell me who you are," he urged.

"My name is Andromeda, the daughter of Cepheus, king of Ethiopia, and I am paying the price of my mother's boastfulness."

"How can that be? Come, tell me."

"My mother's pride in my beauty caused her to declare that I was more beautiful than even the sea-nymphs, lovelier than the queen of the sea herself. So I am to be devoured by the sea monster who carries out the commands of Poseidon, father of the sea."

Even while she spoke the waters turned darker blue, then to a murky blackness as the monster itself rose through the deeps from the sea-bed, fathoms below. Great blood-red barnacles ringed with black glistened along its enormous length. Its jaws gaped wide and its granite-like teeth flashed as it reared its head towards Andromeda.

Without a word and with the speed of light, Perseus flung himself between the girl and the monster and, quickly turning his own head aside, he levered Medusa's head from its wallet and thrust it before the eyes of the deadly creature from the sea.

When the fearful head had been safely returned to the protection of the wallet, he took Andromeda by the hand and turned her eyes to the long, jagged, barnacle-encrusted rock around which dark coils of sea-weed rose and fell with the heaving of the water. No more would that monster cause harm to any living thing.

Perseus held out his hand to the girl, took her in his arms and, with Hermes's sandals, leapt upward to the cliff-top where King Cepheus stood riveted by the drama that had unfolded on the rocky stage below. With singing, feasting and dancing the King and his court celebrated Andromeda's rescue, and feted the hero who had plucked her from the very jaws of the monster.

When Perseus asked Cepheus for his daughter's hand in marriage the feasting began again, and for many days Perseus and his bride enjoyed the tranquillity and the joys of love and marriage.

But the time came to depart. Perseus and his bride set sail for Greece and came at last to the island of Seriphos, seven years after the hero had departed on his quest at the command of Polydectes, who believed that he was rid of Perseus forever.

When Perseus and Andromeda entered the royal hall he saw that Polydectes was still surrounded by the youths who seven years before had jeered and mocked him. Dictys, his one true friend, was in prison; his mother had become a slave of the King.

As Perseus approached, the King looked up insolently and taunted him. "So the hero returns! I see no head of Medusa. Where is the gift I ordered?"

"Here, my lord!"

Averting his own eyes and turning Andromeda aside, Perseus once more withdrew that deadly head from its hiding place. "Here is the gift!"

The King and his guests didn't have time even to gasp. A great silence and a stillness like the coming of ice engulfed the hall. Each man from the King down was carved in stone, for all eyes had turned to the giver and the gift. That tableau Perseus would never forget. King and courtiers grasped goblets not of gold, but of rock. Wine had turned to granite. With the passing years the royal rafters would cave in, walls would crumble, grass would grow around the sculptures, wind and rain would erode their features until today only boulders strew that terrible spot.

On that evening of Perseus's return he set Dictys free and ordered a banquet in honour of his mother. While they feasted Hermes appeared to recover his winged sandals and to return the helmet of invisibility to Hades, the shield to Athena, the sickle to Olympus and the wallet to the Hesperides. He took also the head of Medusa which Athena was to set in the centre of her shield, making it from then on a weapon as well as a defence.

Perseus then proclaimed Dictys king of Seriphos and gladly agreed when Dictys proposed to make Danae his queen. Then he and Andromeda set sail for Argolis where they were to rule for many years, surrounded by their many children.

On their way to Argolis Perseus and Andromeda stopped off at Larissa so that Perseus could compete in the games that the king of that land was holding, for Perseus had already won great renown as a discus thrower, a branch of athletics much admired by the Greeks.

At the games Perseus was the first to throw the discus. The great stadium was hushed as Perseus hurled the iron disc high into the air where it sped across the cleared space, even to where the noble spectators were seated. A cry from the crowd went up as an old man slumped forward, felled by the deadly disc. The old man was Acrisius whose death was instantaneous. He had left Tiryns lest Perseus (on his return) should seek him out to kill him. But the oracle could not be thwarted. Its prophecy was fulfilled and Acrisius was slain by his daughter's son.

Perseus would finally perish after a battle with Dionysus. When he died Zeus set him and Andromeda among the stars, where he remains as an example to all who set their sights on high.

His son Perses was to become king over the Persians, who took their name from him. His granddaughter, Alcmena, would have a son who would one day be known for his muscular strength and his mighty deeds, for his name was Heracles.

Heracles the Strong One

There are more stories about Heracles, who was called Hercules by the Romans, than any other of the Greek heroes. When he was less than a year old, Hera, the wife of almighty Zeus, tried to destroy him by sending two huge writhing serpents to the cradle which he shared with his twin brother, Iphicles. While Iphicles rolled screaming from the cradle Heracles sat up and grasped a snake in each hand, turned away the darting venomous fanged heads and slowly squeezed the reptiles until they were throttled. When his mother and the nurse came running at the sound of Iphicles's screams they found his twin holding out the dead snakes and crowing with delighted satisfaction.

This was only the first of the many evils that Hera tried to bring upon Heracles. Hera's hatred arose out of her jealousy: Zeus was really Heracles's father.

Zeus, lord of Olympus, had greatly desired the beautiful mortal, Alcmena, the granddaughter of Perseus who was married to Amphitryon of Thebes. While Amphitryon was away fighting, the cunning Zeus turned himself and his voice into the likeness of Amphitryon, pretending to have come home from the army to be with Alcmena. Then followed the longest night known to man for Zeus caused the sun to hide and the moon to shine for a night that was really three.

As Amphitryon returned to Thebes Zeus slipped away, but Hera knew that Heracles was conceived by Zeus and only Iphicles was Amphitryon's son. In her rage and jealousy she delayed the birth of Heracles so that Zeus's great-grandson Eurystheus of Mycenae was born before him and would one day be able to claim subservience from Heracles.

Heracles grew to manhood in Thebes. He became renowned for his splendid body, his great physical strength and also for his willingness to help those less strong and able than himself. His education was gained from famous masters.

The grandson of Apollo, Eurytus, taught him the skills of archery, Autolycus showed him how to wrestle and Polydeuces tutored him in the art of fencing. Amphitryon taught him to drive a chariot with skill and grace and saw to it that he learned also the gentle arts: how to read and write and sing. Linus taught him to play upon the lyre.

But one thing Heracles could not control was his temper. Once, when he was but a boy, Linus struck Heracles for playing a false note on the lyre. So forcibly did Heracles retaliate with the instrument in his hand that Linus was killed outright.

For that Heracles was banished to care for cattle on Mount Cithaeron. There he was visited before he was eighteen by two young women who called themselves Pleasure and Virtue. They came to offer him a way of life. Pleasure, whose other name was Vice, tried to lure him with promises of idle luxury free from the labours of body or mind. Virtue promised only toil, tribulation and suffering but in the end true happiness in serving others. That was the path chosen by Heracles.

Even as he made his choice he heard his father's cattle calling and looked up to see a great yellow lion, with murder in its eyes, leaping at the cattle. Before Heracles could reach the creature it had killed one of the cows and disappeared. For fifty days Heracles tracked the beast until he ran it to earth in its foul, evil-smelling lair. With only a club of olive wood and his great strength to defend himself the young hero leapt at the lion, felling it with one almighty blow. So thick and tough was the lion's tawny hide that Heracles's own knife was unable to cut through it when he tried to skin the creature. Only when he cut out one of the razor-sharp claws was he able to skin the hide, which he cured and made into a cloak, with the scalp still attached to be used as a helmet.

His next great deed was to free the city of Thebes from the payment of a heavy tribute being forced from Creon, king of Thebes, by the nearby King Erginus. In gratitude Creon gave Heracles his beautiful daughter, Megara, to be his wife.

All this time Hera jealously waited for an opportunity to do Heracles harm. One day, when his sons and their cousins, the children of Iphicles, were playing together, she sent a fit of madness on Heracles who imagined that Megara and the children were enemies come to destroy Thebes. Fitting an arrow to his bow he fired again and again until he had killed every one of them.

In despair after his madness left him Heracles, banished from his beloved Thebes for murder, and at the command of Zeus, his real father, took himself to Delphi to ask Apollo how best he could atone for the dreadful calamity which had overtaken him.

At Delphi, the voice of the oracle spoke definitely and forcefully: "Go now to Tiryns in Argolis where Eurystheus rules as king. You must serve him faithfully, carrying out to the best of your ability whatever task he requires of you. If you satisfactorily fulfil each labour you will find forgiveness, your soul will be at peace and Zeus himself will raise you to Olympus where you will sit with the Immortals."

Thus began the labours of Heracles . . .

The labours of Heracles

There ruled over Argolis a king who was weak and cowardly. Eurystheus was his name, and he sat in a stone-walled fortress with a huge brazen tower set high at Tiryns. He was secretly jealous of Heracles and hoped that he would be able to bring about the destruction of the hero.

Heracles, still sorrowful over the recent deaths of his wife and children and anxious to make up for the wrong he had done, arrived at the court of Eurystheus. Already he was armed with a club fashioned from the trunk of a wild olive tree, a sword said to be given to him by Hermes, and a bow and arrows received from Apollo.

The mean-minded King lost no time setting Heracles about the first of his trials.

The Nemean lion
The first labour would not take Heracles far from Tiryns. The assignment was to hunt the huge Nemean lion, a monster said to be brother to the Sphinx of Thebes. The Nemean lion had been hurled from the moon and was now ravaging the countryside at Nemea close to Corinth. Each night it descended from the hills, slaying and devouring both beast and man.

"The lion must be killed," decreed Eurystheus, "and you must bring me its skin as proof."

Peasants living in the region warned Heracles that the hide of the lion was so tough that no arrow could pierce it. Indeed, when he strung a sharp-tipped arrow to his bow and sent it flying, the arrow only glanced the fearsome creature and fell harmlessly to the ground.

Unafraid, Heracles stalked the monster to its lair and attacked it with his sword, but that attack proved no more successful than the arrow fired earlier. At last Heracles remembered how, as a youth, he fought the lion at Mount Cithaeron; so he cast aside his sword, stunned the creature momentarily with his club; then wrestled bare-handed with the brute until it rolled over dead, throttled by the hero's mighty arm which he wound tightly around the monster's throat.

With the lion across his shoulders Heracles strode back to Tiryns and flung the carcass at the feet of the quavering King who in horror told him to be off; and should Heracles ever return again from another labour, warned the King, he should remain well outside the fortress.

The hydra of Lerna

Eurystheus then despatched the hero to kill the hydra, a monster who had nine snake-like heads and who lived in the marshes of Lerna near Argos. Many a warrior had tried to kill the hydra, but always as one head was hacked away another grew in its place so that the monster never weakened. One head was said to be immortal and its breath so venomous that it destroyed everything in its path.

Heracles was accompanied on this labour by his nephew Iolaus. The plan was this: Iolaus would keep a great fire burning so that Heracles could fire arrows blazing with bundles of grass into the hydra's cave. The two men set about their task.

As the writhing creature emerged from its cave, Heracles struck it with his sword. But, sure enough, as soon as he dispatched one loathsome head two others even more dreadful grew in its place. Heracles continued to ward off the creature, but even as he parried, a giant crab scurried out of the marsh and attacked him by the feet. Quickly Heracles kicked the crab away and with one almighty blow of his club pounded it to pieces.

At the same time he commanded Iolaus to stand by with a blazing torch. "As I cut off a head so you thrust the torch into the severed neck — quickly!"

This Iolaus did so that no new heads could spring from the stump, and only the immortal head remained. With one final swoop Heracles severed that last and most indomitable head. When this was done, he buried it deep beneath a rock in the barren ground. Before he departed from Lerna, the hero dipped his arrows into the hydra's venom: they would carry that greater potency in future battles.

Heracles returned in triumph to Eurystheus, ready with his good news. But the King wanted to hear none of the victory. Rather, he claimed that Heracles had cheated because he had been helped by Iolaus, and that this labour would not count as Heracles worked toward his forgiveness.

The hind of Ceryneia

"Go now and fetch me alive the hind with the golden horns," commanded the tyrant Eurystheus.

The hind with the golden horns was a magical deer, sacred to Artemis, who wandered free through the region of Oenoe near the Hill of Ceryneia because it was sacrilege to touch it. For over a year Heracles tracked the hind and finally came across it while it slept in Arcadia. As he was taking it to Eurystheus, Artemis, the immortal hunter, turned on him in anger, but when Heracles explained the nature of his task she smiled and told him to take the hind unharmed to Eurystheus.

The boar of Erymanthus

"So much for the golden hind," decreed Eurystheus. "Go once more. This time bring me alive the savage wild boar of Erymanthus."

The boar of which Eurystheus spoke lived on the mountain slopes and terrorised the countryside. This time Heracles set out carrying a stout rope as well as his club.

He quickly came to the tracks of the boar and followed them to a thicket of bushes beyond which lay a huge snow-drift. As Heracles crept from behind the thicket he flung back his head and gave a blood-curdling yell so loud and frightening that the boar suddenly shied away and stumbled into the snow-drift. Quickly binding it with his rope Heracles slung it over his shoulder and, with his load, once more confronted a terrified Eurystheus.

It is said that the King hid in a sunken brass jar, he was so afraid of what he saw. But he soon emerged to send the hero on yet another task.

Cleaning the Augean stables

"This is a task you will not enjoy. Get yourself to Elis where King Augeas lives. He owns the largest herd of cattle in the whole of Greece, but his stables have not been cleaned in thirty years. They stink. Go clean them—and do so in one day."

Heracles found the stables to be as filthy as they had been described. They were waist high in foul-smelling dung which spread pestilence as well as a bad odour. Although Augeas was happy for Heracles to do his dirty work he warned him that one barrow load alone would take an hour, and surely it would take at least a thousand hours to clean the stables.

"If I do it," bargained Heracles, "will you give me a tenth of your herd in repayment?"

"So be it," answered the King.

Then Heracles built a dam across the nearby swiftly running river, Alpheus, and diverted the waters so that when the cattle were out grazing and the doors of the stables were opened wide, a great gush of water came flooding through, swirling away the dirt and dung of thirty years.

But A⋯ ⋯ised to honour his bargain and it was only years later that
He⋯ ⋯o punish him. Eurystheus, too, claimed that this labour would
⋯ Heracles had demanded payment; so the King set him yet

⋯us

⋯halian birds. They belong to Ares, and they live in the
⋯e of Stymphalus. They have claws of brass and they
⋯ttack and eat all who pass by."

⋯racles was met by Athena who warned him that the
⋯could pierce the stoutest armour. She gave him,
⋯de of bronze fashioned by Hephaestus.

⋯ugh the forest gloom he heard the squawking of
⋯astanets he sprang through the trees setting up
⋯flew off shrieking. Although he was able to
⋯ned arrows others escaped to the island of
⋯aging with the Argonauts, Heracles was to

The⋯

Unin⋯ ⋯ow ordered Heracles to Crete. "Bring
me ba⋯ ⋯rete, father of the terrible Minotaur,
half ma⋯

Herac⋯ ⋯at Crete, he found his way to the
great pal⋯ ⋯self known to King Minos who
promised a⋯ ⋯e the bull.

Heracles, ⋯ong of limb and swift of foot,
needed no he⋯ ⋯t on the run and some say that
he swam back⋯ ⋯t when he offered it alive to
Eurystheus the⋯ ⋯nto his brazen hiding place,
cowering in fear. ⋯d the Isthmus of Corinth to
the fields of Mar⋯ ⋯another hero, Theseus, conquered it.

The horses of Diom⋯

When Eurystheus rec⋯ ⋯ed from his fright he set Heracles his eighth labour.
"You must now journey north and bring me back the horses of King Diomedes."

These animals belonged to the king of Thrace and were four mares which he
fed on the human flesh of those conquered in battle. They were certainly terrible
to behold. When he was not at war Diomedes fed them the flesh of his guests

whose throats were cut and whose bodies were placed in the palace mangers. If Heracles was to take the horses back to Tiryns he had first of all to escape the fate of other royal guests.

All his first night at the palace in Thrace he lay sleepless. As the long night drew to a close, he rose before dawn and crept to the stables while the sentries and grooms still slept. There Heracles saw the four mares chained in their stalls, and nearby a great axe. Swiftly, Heracles burst the staples holding the chains and drove the terrified horses from the stables on to the high ground of an inlet surrounded on three sides by the sea. With sweeping strokes he cut a channel on the land side of the peninsula, making an island on which the horses were trapped. As Diomedes and his guards approached, the hero attacked and dispatched them with his axe, then threw the bodies across to the mares who devoured the human flesh and at once became strangely docile. Heracles had no trouble in binding their jaws with stout cord before taking them on board ship and setting sail for Tiryns.

The girdle of the Amazon queen

Heracles now faced his ninth labour.

"You must bring me the golden girdle of Hippolyta, queen of the Amazons, for my daughter Admete," commanded Eurystheus.

The Amazons were a war-like race of women who lived by the Black Sea. The golden girdle which gave its wearer strength in battle had been given to Hippolyta by Ares, the god of war, himself, and was finely and intricately wrought.

It was a long journey but Heracles arrived safely. After he explained his mission to the Amazon Queen she gladly offered him the girdle, because she knew of his exploits.

But the interfering Hera once more caused trouble for Heracles, spreading the lie that he really wanted to seize Hippolyta and carry her off. This made Queen Hippolyta angry and she called the Amazons to war. With his strength and ingenuity, Heracles was able to more than defend himself. But in the skirmish Hippolyta was killed. So it was with sorrow in his heart that Heracles took the girdle and sailed once more for Argolis where he presented Eurystheus with the prize.

The cattle of Geryon

The last three labours of Heracles were long and arduous, and they were to take him beyond the boundaries of the then-known world.

"Do not return until you drive before you the cattle which belong to Geryon and which are guarded by the herdsman Eurytion and his two-headed monstrous guard-dog, Orthrus," spat Eurystheus. Geryon, who was the king of Tartessus in Spain, was a three-headed monster who had two legs but three pairs of arms and hands.

To reach Spain, Heracles borrowed from Helios the golden "goblet of the sun", which was shaped like a giant water lily and in which Helios the sun god himself sailed each evening to his palace at the other side of the ocean.

As he passed through the strait that separates Spain from Africa, Heracles set up two great stone pillars, one at Gibraltar and one at Ceuta. These are known even today as the Pillars of Heracles.

Then he travelled overland to Tartessus where he quickly dispatched the two-headed guard-dog with one arrow and the herdsman with another. As he began to drive the cattle away Geryon himself took up the pursuit. Heracles hid behind a bush until the ogre appeared, then he fired from the side, piercing the giant's three throats with one arrow, so mighty was his thrust.

He then herded the cattle into the golden bowl and sailed back to Helios to whom he returned this wondrous vessel. From Spain he had the task of driving the cattle overland to Greece—a long weary journey beset with many dangers and adventures including a battle with the fire-breathing troll, Cacus. It was a nearly exhausted hero who eventually arrived in Tiryns and handed over the cattle to Eurystheus, his tenth labour satisfactorily completed.

The golden apples of the Hesperides

The relentless Eurystheus, however, gave Heracles no rest. "You must now bring me three golden apples from the garden of the Hesperides," he commanded.

With a sigh of resignation Heracles went on his way. He travelled first to Illyria where he begged the nymphs who lived there to tell him where he could find the garden of the Hesperides; but all they could tell him was that he must travel to Mount Caucasus and ask Prometheus, who was chained there by Zeus in punishment for bringing fire to mankind. As a further punishment to Prometheus, a great eagle came each day to pluck at his liver.

Even as Heracles approached the chained Titan, he heard the awful fluttering of the eagle's wings. While it hovered ready to attack, Heracles loosed one of his poisoned arrows and the great bird plunged screaming into the Black Sea, thousands of feet below. With his sword Heracles hacked away the fetters by which Prometheus was bound and the Titan, after many years of suffering and torment, was free once more.

"I am Heracles, son of Zeus, who set you free, but my father bids me tell you that hereafter you must wear a ring on your finger as a symbol of the metal fetters which bound you all these years."

From that day onward mankind has worn rings in memory of the sufferings of

33

Prometheus—who now turned to Heracles and spoke.

"The tree you seek grows in a magic garden at the world's end, on the slopes of the mountain where my brother Atlas crouches forever supporting the heavens upon his shoulders. In the garden dwell the immortal daughters of Hesperus, the evening star, who is the son of Atlas; but around the tree is curled the dragon Ladon, guardian of the apples."

It was a long adventuresome journey that took Heracles to Mount Atlas, where the Titan held up the sky lest it crush the earth. From the mountain top Heracles could look down into the glades and gardens of Paradise where the nymphs of Hesperus sang as they danced through shady glens and around the tree with its gleaming golden apples.

"First you must slay the dragon," warned Atlas. Once again Heracles sped an arrow from his trusted bow and pierced the throat of the monster whose blue and gold scales were like shining armour.

"Now I will go to my daughters who will fetch the apples for you," said Atlas, "so you must relieve me of my burden while I am away."

"Can't I go myself?" asked Heracles.

"No. It would take you many days. Only I know where to find the nymphs. Only they can pluck the apples."

So Heracles took Atlas's heavy load, and while he held high the heavens, Atlas descended to the garden. Impatient hours passed before Atlas returned with the glittering fruit, which he held tantalisingly toward Heracles.

"Why don't I take them to Eurystheus myself? I deserve a holiday, and you are a strong fellow and can easily support the sky!" he cunningly suggested.

"But before you go," interrupted Heracles, "this burden sits uncomfortably on my shoulders, which are unused to the task. Hold it for me while I take up a more comfortable position. I'll hold the apples while you get into position."

Atlas leaned forward and bent his shoulders so Heracles could transfer his load. When the sky was once more in its accustomed place Heracles set off briskly down the mountain side. Atlas had been tricked and his short holiday was over.

Yet again Heracles returned to Tiryns, having completed his eleventh labour.

The dog Cerberus

"You have conquered the world, get you now to the Underworld, to Hades, whose entrance is guarded by Cerberus, the fiercest hound ever spawned. Your task is to bring Cerberus back to me, alive." Thus spoke Eurystheus.

Down through a deep gloomy cavern in Sparta, through the jaws of Hell, travelled Heracles with Hermes as his guide—for part of Hermes's duties was to lead lost souls to Hades.

At the River Styx, Charon, the ferryman, was hesitant. His passengers were always dead souls who paid him a coin, which they carried in their mouth. But Hermes badgered the boatman and Heracles frowned fiercely so that the old man took up his oars in spite of his doubt, and rowed across the river to Hades.

There Heracles walked through gloom and blackness, encountered terrible sights, and was attacked by dreadful sounds exuding from wraith-like ghosts who moaned and gibbered, like the gorgon Medusa who had been slain by Perseus. At last he came to the Underworld where Hades and Persephone sat upon their thrones. Heracles begged leave of them to borrow Cerberus and take him back to Eurystheus.

"Only if you can overcome him without using your weapons," they told him, for Cerberus had three heads, a mane of hissing snakes and a serpent for a tail.

Thinking back to his first labour Heracles quickly whipped from his shoulders the skin of the Nemean lion which he flung around the fearsome dog, entangling its heads in its folds. He then gathered the brute into his arms and set off, back across the dark river of Styx, up through the caverns to the world of sunlight and fresh breezes. In triumph he entered Tiryns, and the presence of the King.

"My labours are at an end. Take your dog!" he cried, and threw the hound at Eurystheus, which rushed forward snarling and hissing. The terrified King screamed and hid once more in his jar until Heracles gathered up the dog and set out again for the Underworld, where he delivered Cerberus safely back to Hades.

The labours of Heracles were over. It was on his way home that he visited his friend Pittheus, who had a grandson about seven years old. When the boy saw the skin of the Nemean lion that Heracles had thrown over a chair, he took up a sword and attacked it, thinking it was alive. Laughingly, Heracles caught up the boy in his arms.

"What is your name, my young hero?"

"Why, Theseus, sir, and one day I shall indeed be called Hero." And so it was to be.

Although the labours of Heracles were at an end, his wars and adventures continued many and varied. He fought in Troy, returned to King Augeas to demand payment for the cleaning of the stables, and sailed with Jason when he set out to capture the golden fleece.

Late in his life he married Deianeira, sister of his friend Meleager. When a centaur named Nessus attempted to carry off Deianeira, Heracles killed the centaur with an arrow. In his dying moments Nessus told Deianeira to soak some linen in his blood and make it into a tunic. If ever Heracles ceased to love her all she had to do was to get him to wear this garment.

Some years later Deianeira heard of Heracles's infatuation with a young maiden so when Heracles asked his wife to send him a new tunic because he wished to consecrate an altar to Zeus, she sent him the one impregnated with the blood of Nessus. As soon as Heracles put on the garment the poisoned blood seared his flesh and caused intolerable pain; but it was stuck firmly to his skin, and he was unable to tear it away.

When Deianeira realised what had happened she killed herself in despair. Heracles, knowing that his time had come, made one magnificent final effort. He climbed to the top of Mount Oeta where he built a funeral pyre, laid himself across the self-made altar and commanded his attendants to set it aflame. As the pyre blazed high into the sky thunder pealed from above and Heracles was caught up into the heavens to become one of the Immortals; the long years of enmity with Hera finally over.

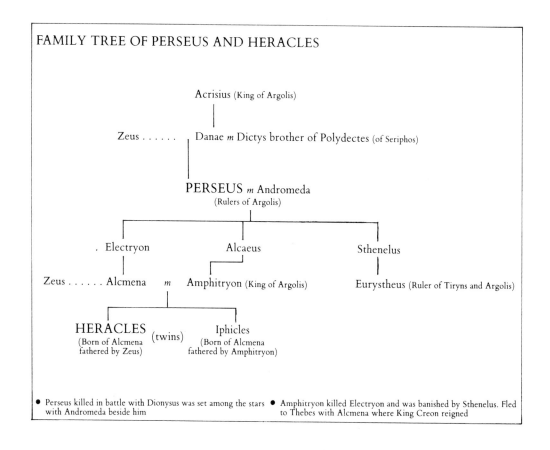

FAMILY TREE OF PERSEUS AND HERACLES

Acrisius (King of Argolis)

Zeus . . . . . . Danae *m* Dictys brother of Polydectes (of Seriphos)

PERSEUS *m* Andromeda
(Rulers of Argolis)

. Electryon   Alcaeus   Sthenelus

Zeus . . . . . . Alcmena   *m*   Amphitryon (King of Argolis)   Eurystheus (Ruler of Tiryns and Argolis)

HERACLES (twins) Iphicles
(Born of Alcmena   (Born of Alcmena
fathered by Zeus)   fathered by Amphitryon)

● Perseus killed in battle with Dionysus was set among the stars with Andromeda beside him   ● Amphitryon killed Electryon and was banished by Sthenelus. Fled to Thebes with Alcmena where King Creon reigned

Theseus the Daring and the Bold

King Aegeus of Athens had not been able to have children by any of his wives, so he consulted the oracle at Delphi. He was instructed to visit the king of Troezen who had a daughter called Aethra; and Aegeus fell in love with her.

They would have a son who would be called Theseus, but before he was born Aegeus had to return to Athens. Before he left he summoned six strong men and ordered them to lever aside a huge boulder that towered above the plains outside the city. While the men held the great rock poised on the brink of the crater beneath, Aegeus took his sandals and his sword and placed them in the hole. Then he commanded the boulder to be lowered carefully into place again.

"When Theseus grows to manhood," he told Aethra, "he will have the strength of an ox. He will be able to move aside the boulder, recover my sword and sandals and come to me at Athens. I will know that it is Theseus when I see these tokens."

Theseus's childhood was that of a real hero. He grew up strong and fearless, learning to be a true man from his grandfather, and learning grace and strength of will from his mother. When Heracles visited the court he recognised an heroic spirit.

When Theseus turned eighteen he said to his mother, "The time has come for me to go to my father and become the king of Athens."

"But not until you have recovered your father's sword and sandals," warned Aethra. So she led him out to the plain and showed him the boulder, explaining its secret.

With iron resolve and with muscles rippling, Theseus gathered his strength and rolled away the stone as though it were a marble. This was his initiation into manhood. This manhood he was to prove again and again on the long and arduous overland journey to Athens, a journey during which robbers, bandits and monsters lay in wait.

His first trial came at Epidaurus where Periphetes the Clubman lay in wait to batter travellers to death with his iron-tipped club. The monster was no match for Theseus, who wrestled with him until he was able to gain possession of the club and give the muscle man the punishment he deserved.

On the Isthmus of Corinth Theseus encountered Sinis, called the Pinebender, who used to bind travellers to two bent pine saplings, one leg fastened to each sapling. He would then catapult his victim through the air. But Theseus tied down the ruffian giant in the same way and repaid him with his own medicine.

Next he met Sciron, along where the path from Megara to Athens follows the coast. High above the sea Sciron lay in wait demanding toll from passers-by — whom he forced to wash his feet. As they bent to do so, Sciron would kick them swiftly over the cliff-edge into the swirling waters below.

Theseus was ready for Sciron. "I pay toll to no man," he told him, and as Sciron kicked out viciously Theseus sidestepped, caught Sciron's foot and hurled him over his shoulder and into the sea where he was devoured by the enormous turtle to which he had fed travellers for so long.

Further along the coast Theseus reached Eleusis where the gigantic wrestler Cercyon challenged him to combat, as he did with all wayfarers. His brute strength enabled him to crush his opponents in a bear-like hug. But Theseus was stronger and much speedier. His lithe body darted and coiled until the giant's legs were pinned beneath him. Then Theseus raised Cercyon bodily and dashed him, lifeless, to the ground.

Finally Theseus arrived at the tower of Procrustes, who provided hospitality for passers-by. In the tower was a bed which Procrustes offered his guests. But in the dead of night Procustes would steal into the chamber. If the sleeper was too tall for the bed he would cut off his legs, but if he was too short, he would use the bed as a rack and stretch his victim violently until he fitted the bed exactly.

When he offered Theseus the bed the hero took hold of the villain and dumped him on to his own bed. First he cut off his feet and then his head, until Procrustes was made to fit his own bed perfectly.

So Theseus cleared the highway of peril for future travellers. Finally, he arrived in Athens and made his way to the royal palace. But his father was under the spell of Medea, a witch-wife who recognised Theseus and was afraid that King Aegeus would take away favour from her own son Medus.

Medea cunningly arranged a banquet that night for the young stranger, planning to poison his wine and tell Aegeus that his son had come to murder him. Aegeus, for his part, dispatched the traveller, about whom such wondrous tales were told, to slay the bull which Heracles had brought from Crete and which now marauded the plains of Marathon, terrorising and killing.

The young Theseus boldly faced the Cretan bull, grasped it by the horns and dragged it back to the city where, at the Acropolis, he offered it as a sacrifice to Athena.

That night at the feast prepared by Medea, as Medea was handing him the goblet of poisoned wine, Theseus drew his sword to carve up the remains of the Cretan bull. As he raised the goblet to his lips, Aegeus's eye fell on the sword in his other hand and recognised it as his own; then he saw his sandals on his son's feet. When he embraced Theseus the goblet dashed to the ground and the searing venom in the wine hissed as it ate its way through the paving.

With great joy Aegeus received his son. He sent Medea into exile and pronounced Theseus his heir and successor.

Theseus and the Minotaur

When King Aegeus proclaimed Theseus the next king of Athens, his nephews, the sons of Pallas, were upset and angry. They determined that Theseus would not gain the throne so they divided into two groups determined to ambush the young prince. Theseus, however, was warned by a herald called Leos. He gathered an army of Athenians, marched against his enemies and massacred them.

Rather than finding Athens joyful over their hero's triumph, Theseus returned to find the city plunged into gloom. The Athenians grieved because the regular envoys from Crete had arrived to demand their annual tribute of seven youths and seven maidens. This yearly tribute was to avenge the death of Androgeus, the King's son, who had been one of the victims of the great bull at Marathon. The youths and maidens were to be taken to Crete and imprisoned in a huge labyrinthine maze at Knossus built by Daedalus and inhabited by the Minotaur, a monster half man and half bull born from the union of Pasiphaë, wife of King Minos of Crete, and Poseidon, the sea-god. The monster lived in the very centre of the labyrinth, in a corridor hedged about with thorns. Its horns were as sharp as knives and no one had ever escaped its attack. Any sacrificial victim who managed to hide and was not devoured by the Minotaur became hopelessly lost in the maze and slowly starved to death.

Theseus at once offered to go to Crete as one of the seven young men, and would not be dissuaded by the pleading of his father.

"Did I not capture the bull of Marathon after my most dangerous journey from Troezen to Athens? If I can slay the Minotaur and put an end to this terrible tribute, I will; otherwise I shall perish myself."

"So be it," said his father sadly. "But make me a promise: if you return to Athens in safety, sail with the white sails of victory so that I will know as soon as I see the ship that you are safe!" He said this because it was the custom to rig the ship that carried the young men and women doomed to die with black sails of mourning, both for the outward voyage to Crete and the sad return. This Theseus promised to do, and he took his place among the sacrificial seven.

In Crete the party was met by Minos and his beautiful daughter, Ariadne, who was smitten on sight by the heroic good looks, grace and noble bearing of Theseus. There and then she determined that he should not die.

That night she visited Daedalus, the designer of the maze, and asked him for help. Daedalus was loath to help as he himself had been banished from Athens but, after binding Ariadne to secrecy, he told her that as fearful as the Minotaur was, it could be overcome by a hero brave enough to conquer his fear of the hideous sight and fight the monster. But to find a way out of the maze was perhaps an even greater problem, and here Daedalus bowed low and whispered into the maiden's ear.

Ariadne glided through the great palace and stole silently into the bedchamber of Theseus. "If I help you," she whispered, "promise that you will take me with you back to Athens and marry me, for my life would be worthless if it were discovered that I had aided you." This Theseus promised. Ariadne then unfolded her plan.

In the morning Theseus volunteered to go first into the labyrinth. Hidden in his hand was a ball of thread given to him by Ariadne. As the great door of the prison was closing behind him, Theseus managed to fasten the free end of the thread to the doorpost. Then he rolled the ball forward, following it as it led him through the dark winding passages to the centre of the maze where the Minotaur pawed the ground, bellowing its hungry defiance at this mortal who dared to challenge him. Theseus resolutely looked the brute straight in the eye as it glared at him through the thorny thicket. The ground seemed to give way under its feet when it charged, its lance-like horns glinting in the half-light.

Nimbly Theseus dodged the attack and as the Minotaur thundered by he smote it a mighty blow to the heart with his fist. Again it charged, and again Theseus danced aside and punched. Time and again he pounded until the creature was dazed and began to flag. Then the mighty arm of Theseus wrapped around its neck and his free hand grasped at the base of one of the horns. He wrenched and twisted as the bull writhed in anger and torment. At last the horn was wrested from its socket, with the snap of broken bone and torn gristle. With a sword-like thrust Theseus drove the razor-sharp horn into the Minotaur's own throat. As Ariadne had predicted, the monster was killed with the very weapon that had caused the death of so many others.

As soon as he recovered his breath Theseus looked around and picked up the thread which had led him so accurately through the maze. Rewinding it into a ball, he retraced his steps until he reached the doorpost where the end was tied. Ariadne waited there while the guards dozed at their post. Swiftly and silently, but with the confidence of knowing the way, she led Theseus and the other intended victims to the port where their ship lay off shore. As they lifted the anchor and the rigged sails filled with wind, the guards awoke and sounded the alarm.

Minos, who was not at heart a tyrant, was not unhappy that the Minotaur had been slain, but he was furious at the flight of Ariadne. Knowing that her help could only have come from Daedalus he incarcerated the craftsman and his son Icarus in the labyrinth which Daedalus had designed. (The tale of this pair's great escape from the maze is another story.)

Theseus and Ariadne were safe and full sails winged them towards Athens. As the ship sped along, their love increased, and they spent their days planning a life together. Their happiness grew with each setting of the sun.

Then one night as Theseus slept on deck with the sea scudding by he had a dream that not he but Dionysus, the god of wine and ecstasy, would marry his beloved Ariadne. To Theseus this was both prophecy and fate. That fate soon became reality.

Shortly, the ship called at the island of Naxos and the entire company went ashore at a place where Dionysus and his satyrs were feasting and dancing. As Ariadne walked through the woods Dionysus saw her beauty and, wanting her for his wife, he cast upon her a spell of heavenly sleep so that when she awoke she forgot all about Theseus and accepted the proposal of Dionysus.

Theseus returned to his ship despondent and so full of grief at the loss of Ariadne that he withdrew more and more into himself. As the ship sailed through the Gulf of Aegina and approached Athens he was unaware that his father Aegeus stood anxiously on the Acropolis, peering seaward for sight of a white sail. In his despondency Theseus had forgotten his promise; the ship's sails were black against the blue of the sea.

Looking down from where he stood, Aegeus saw this as a symbol of mourning. Despairing at the supposed loss of his son, he dashed himself to his death from the heights of the Acropolis to the rocks below. So even today, that sea of sadness is called the Aegean.

Theseus was to rule Athens for many years and was recognised as a just and wise king who brought peace to his land and helped build a prosperous and well-governed city.

However, his adventures were not over. When Jason called for volunteers to sail in search of the golden fleece, Theseus eagerly joined the expedition.

When Athens was invaded by the Amazons, Theseus fought them off and married their leader, Hippolyta, by whom he had a son, Hippolytus. Later Theseus divorced Hippolyta and, after hearing that Minos of Crete was dead, made peace with the new king and married Ariadne's sister, Phaedra.

Toward the end of his life trouble broke out in the city and a rebellious faction drove Theseus into exile on the island of Skyros. King Lycomedes pretended to welcome him but murdered him by casting him into the sea from a high mountain.

Many years later the oracle at Delphi told of the bones of a hero buried on Skyros. When the Athenians dug up the bones they discovered the sword and sandals that had belonged to Aegeus. So they knew that the remains belonged to Theseus. These they took home to Athens and Theseus was at last buried in the city which he loved and over which he had ruled.

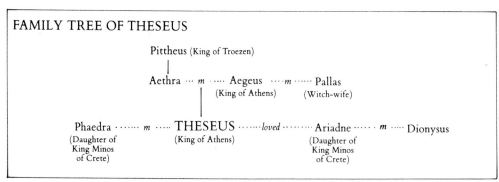

FAMILY TREE OF THESEUS

Pittheus (King of Troezen)

Aethra ···· m ····· Aegeus ····· m ····· Pallas
(King of Athens)   (Witch-wife)

Phaedra ········ m ····· THESEUS ······ loved ········ Ariadne ······ m ····· Dionysus
(Daughter of   (King of Athens)   (Daughter of
King Minos   King Minos
of Crete)   of Crete)

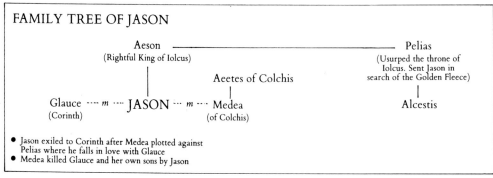

FAMILY TREE OF JASON

Aeson ———————————————————— Pelias
(Rightful King of Iolcus)   (Usurped the throne of
                                             Iolcus. Sent Jason in
                      Aeetes of Colchis   search of the Golden Fleece)

Glauce ···· m ···· JASON ··· m ··· Medea   Alcestis
(Corinth)   (of Colchis)

- Jason exiled to Corinth after Medea plotted against Pelias where he falls in love with Glauce
- Medea killed Glauce and her own sons by Jason

Jason the Voyager

In ancient Greece there was a fair and noble youth named Jason whose father, the rightful king of Iolcus, had been driven from his throne by the tyrant Pelias. The deposed King carried his son to a mountain cave where lived the wise and kindly centaur, Chiron, who was man to the waist but below that possessed the body of a noble horse. Many kings sent their sons to Chiron to be trained as hero-princes. Jason became skilled in riding, hunting and wrestling yet was an able musician, singer and dancer. He also became known as "the healer" because of his knowledge of medicine.

When he felt that Chiron had taught him all that he needed to know, Jason set out for Iolcus to demand of Pelias his father's kingdom. On the way he had to ford a raging river. An old woman on the bank asked the young man to ferry her across on his shoulders. Jason responded warmly but it was a difficult crossing. As he struggled up the further bank he discovered that he had lost one of the richly embroidered sandals he was wearing that had belonged to his father.

When he set the old woman down he was astonished to find that she had changed into a shining goddess—Hera, the wife of the almighty Zeus. Before she vanished Hera promised Jason that if he always spoke as she bade, he would become one of the most famous heroes of Greece.

With this promise held in his heart, Jason limped into the city of Iolcus where folk began to whisper, "The man with one sandal has come!"

Jason, the Argonauts and the golden fleece

Many years before Jason's arrival in Iolcus, the usurper king of the city had been warned by the oracle that a youth with but one sandal would cause his death. When Pelias learnt that the stranger had arrived, and that it was his nephew

Jason, he pretended to be pleased and welcomed him, saying, "I need such a man as you to be my counsellor. But first you must journey to Colchis and bring me back the golden fleece. Then I shall willingly yield my throne to you, my nephew."

Now Jason knew all about the fleece of gold that had come from the great ram and hung from the branch of a great ilex tree in Colchis, shedding its yellow light far abroad. He knew, too, that it was guarded by a sleepless dragon and that many heroes had perished as they tried to snatch it away.

Yet he resolved to go forth and win the fleece, provided that on his return his uncle promised to restore the kingdom to his father. So he went to Argus, the famous shipbuilder, and asked him to build a galley with fifty oars, after which he dispatched messengers throughout the land calling for young kings and princes to join him in his quest. First came Heracles, then Theseus from Athens, Atalanta the huntress, Orpheus the musician: in all forty-nine zealous and youthful heroes.

When the heroes were gathered at Iolcus they drew the great galley, the *Argo*, down to the beach on rollers. Then, as Orpheus played gently on his lyre, the *Argo* rolled into the sea.

Northward they sailed. Before braving the perils of the Black Sea they stopped at the cave of Colchis to receive the blessing of the wise old man. Fogs and ice-cold storms beset them, but most dangerous of all were the dreaded Wandering Rocks, or Clashers as they were known, rocks that actually moved and clashed together with a noise louder than thunder. It seemed to the Argonauts that they would never get through without being crushed. Then they saw a dove — sent by Hera to Jason to act as his pilot. The dove hovered above the troubled sea, then darted through the chasm just as the rocks were closing together. The heroes saw her pass through unhurt except for one tail feather, caught as the Clashers met with a grinding crash. As the rocks parted the heroes strained at the oars and the *Argo* flew through the channel straight as an arrow to safety.

On sailed the Argonauts until they spied ahead the gleaming gold of the palace of King Aeëtes, in the city of Colchis where deep in the woods in a sacred grove hung the fabled golden fleece.

Although Aeëtes pretended to welcome Jason and his Argonauts he was secretly angry. "I will let you have the golden fleece," he said, "if you can yoke my bulls which breathe fire from their nostrils, plough a four-acre field with them, and sow it with dragons' teeth!"

That night, as Jason sat sadly wondering how he could possibly fulfil such a task, he was summoned to the palace by a messenger of Medea, the King's beautiful daughter, an enchantress who had fallen at first sight in love with Jason.

"If you trust me," she said, "and you are indeed without fear, I shall help you do as the King commands. Here is an ointment made from a magic flower. Anoint your body and you shall have the strength of seven men and neither fire nor sword shall harm you." Then, as she handed him a basket containing the dragons' teeth, she said, "Now promise me that when you take the fleece and sail back to Greece, you will take me with you as your wife." And Jason promised.

The next morning Jason anointed himself and, to the astonishment and anger of the King, he yoked the bulls without harm, ploughed the field and sowed it with dragons' teeth. But immediately they were sown the teeth began to grow and up sprang an army of men ready to attack.

"Throw in among them the basket which contained the teeth," urged Medea. As soon as this was done the warriors began to fight among themselves until they all lay dead.

When all was over Aeëtes turned to Jason, "Tomorrow, the golden fleece is yours."

But that night Medea came to Jason with a warning that the King was plotting to slay him. She led Jason and Orpheus through the night to the sacred grove where the fleece glowed in its golden splendour. Jason called out with joy and wonder but was halted in his eager rush forward by the sight of the hideous guardian dragon, dull-skinned, foul-spotted and with lank, rusty hair about his neck.

"Play your lyre and sing the melody," whispered Medea to Orpheus, and she herself began to murmur a spell. Then as Orpheus began to sing his "Hymn to Sleep" in a low sweet voice, the grove itself became enfolded in a drowsy stillness. Jason remained awake only because of the magic ointment with which Medea had covered him. As the dreaded monster closed its eyes in a trance-like sleep and its great body became motionless, Medea sprinkled its length with a magic potion. Then Jason glided forward, climbed gracefully along and up the coils of its back and into the ilex tree where the golden fleece hung. "Hurry," urged Medea, "my spell cannot hold the dragon for much longer."

Triumphantly, Jason grasped the fleece of gold and by the light that it shed he, Orpheus and Medea sped through the gloom of the garden, along secret paths to the water's edge where the *Argo* was beached. The anchor was weighed and as the long oars stirred the water, the galley slid down river to the open sea even as Aeëtes and his men shot poisoned arrows in rage at the scudding Argonauts. In the sacred grove, the dragon awoke from its charmed sleep and hissed with rage at the loss of the fleece.

The Argonauts fended off the arrows with their shields and Orpheus, taking up his lyre, sang a triumphant song of praise to the heroes. To this music Jason and his heroes, with the enchantress Medea, turned towards Iolcus to claim the kingdom for the proud possessor of the golden fleece and his bride.

Odysseus: Agile of Body and Mind

The blind Greek poet, Homer, who is thought to have lived between six and seven hundred years before the birth of Christ, featured Odysseus as a hero figure in both the *Iliad* and *Odyssey*. Both works are long epic poems telling the story of the Trojan war and what happened afterwards. Odysseus took part in the war and is one of many characters in the *Iliad*. The *Odyssey* is actually a novel-like account of his wanderings after the war on his long journey home.

Odysseus was the son of Laertes, king of the rocky northern island of Ithaca in the Peloponnesus, the southern peninsula of the country we now call Greece. Although Odysseus was not handsome, but almost grizzly, he was both strong and stalwart and had a cunning wit that made him one of the most astute of ancient heroes.

As a youth he heard talk of the most beautiful of women, Helen, daughter of Tyndareus, king of Sparta. So he sailed to Sparta and joined the many suitors who sought Helen's hand in marriage. But while at the court he fell in love with Penelope, a cousin to Helen, who looked favourably upon him despite his plain appearance.

Odysseus went to King Tyndareus and suggested that the King should require all the suitors to swear an oath to bide by the King's decision before he announced which one of them would marry Helen. Tyndareus saw the wisdom of Odysseus's suggestion and chose Menelaus, the brave young prince of Mycenae, to marry Helen. In gratitude to Odysseus for his wise suggestion, the King persuaded his brother, Icarius, to allow Odysseus to marry his daughter Penelope.

The cause of the Trojan war is a fascinating story. It came about that King Priam of Troy was warned by a soothsayer that his son, Paris, would disrupt the fair country and bring disaster to it. Priam then banished Paris from the kingdom and sent him to tend his sheep on Mount Ida. There Paris lived with the nymph Oenone.

50

It was while Paris was living on Mount Ida that a quarrel broke out among the gods and goddesses of Mount Olympus. Eris, the goddess of discord, was not invited to the wedding feast of King Peleus and the sea-nymph, Thetis. Eris became furiously angry and threw a golden apple marked "For the Fairest of All" into the banquet hall. There was much bickering among the dwellers of Mount Olympus and only after a great deal of quarrelling were all but three goddesses eliminated from the contest. Left were Hera, Pallas Athena, and Aphrodite. These goddesses went to Zeus and demanded that he judge which of them was the fairest.

Zeus was too shrewd to make such a decision, knowing that he could only please one of them. He told them to go to Mount Ida and ask Paris, who was said to be an excellent judge of beauty.

When the three beautiful goddesses appeared before Paris with their request he was dumbfounded. In his eyes each was more beautiful than the other. The goddesses offered him bribes. Hera promised him the kingship of Europe and Asia; Athena promised that Troy under his leadership would defeat the Greeks; Aphrodite, more cunning than her sisters, promised him the fairest woman in the world for himself.

So it was to Aphrodite that Paris gave the golden apple: "For the Fairest of All". This judgement was to spark the Trojan war, for at that time the fairest mortal in the world was Helen, now married to Menelaus of Sparta who was brother to Agamemnon, the overlord of much of Greece.

Aphrodite conducted Paris to the court of Helen and Menelaus. There he was graciously received and treated royally. After some time Menelaus, trusting Paris completely, left on an expedition for Crete. Paris at once pressed his suit with Helen and when she was willing, bore her off to Troy.

Menelaus immediately rallied an army to go and bring Helen back. He called in all the Greek chieftains to aid him and appointed Agamemnon commander-in-chief. Only two warriors were missing — Odysseus and Achilles.

Odysseus, who was one of the shrewdest and most sensible men in Greece, and who now had a son named Telemachus, was unhappy about leaving his home and family. So he pretended to be insane by ploughing up the seashore and throwing salt in the furrows. When the messenger of Agamemnon, who was well aware of how cunning Odysseus could be, placed the baby Telemachus in front of the plough Odysseus had to give up his pretence of insanity and turn the plough aside. Thus he was forced to join the army.

Achilles believed that if he went to Troy he would die before the war was over. Although he disguised himself in women's clothing Odysseus recognised him and summoned him to join the army. Knowing that destiny must be fulfilled, Achilles went off with Odysseus to fight against the Trojans.

In the long years that Troy was under seige Odysseus proved himself to be a brave and crafty warrior. He it was who stole the statue of the goddess, which was called the Palladium, from the Temple of Athena, because he had been told of the ancient prophecy which said that Troy could never be taken while the statue remained in the Temple. It was Odysseus, too, who slipped into the city disguised as a beggar to spy out the land, and whose cunning mind devised the great wooden horse which eventually gave the Greeks access to the city and led to the sacking of Troy.

After Troy had fallen Odysseus was anxious to return to his beloved Penelope and his island kingdom, so he lost no time in assembling his men and ships for the perilous voyage back to Ithaca. That journey is now known as the Odyssey and, in spite of Athena's protection which had always been his, Odysseus was to spend nineteen long, weary years, brave many dangers, undergo strange adventures and lose many sailors before sighting his island home again.

Indeed, although the other Greek heroes who took part in the war had been allowed to return home, Odysseus had by order of Poseidon — the god of the sea and whom he had offended — been detained, a prisoner of the nymph Calypso. Only after a conference of the gods did Zeus decree that Odysseus be allowed to return home to Ithaca. Zeus sent Hermes, the messenger of the gods, to Calypso with orders to release Odysseus. When the nymph reluctantly agreed to the decree, Odysseus built a boat in four days and quickly sailed away from his island prison.

But Poseidon, always the enemy of Odysseus, sent a great wind to destroy his boat and to wash him ashore on the coast of the Phaeacians. He was found there by Nausicaa, daughter of King Alcinous of the Phaeacians, when she went with her handmaidens to the mouth of the river to wash linen. The cries of Nausicaa and her women woke Odysseus from an exhausted sleep. The hero, realising that he was naked, broke a leafy bough behind which to hide and advanced upon the women like a mountain lion in the prime of his power. Even so, his naked body grimed with salt made a gruesome sight and the maidens ran away in alarm. All but Nausicaa, who stood her ground and asked Odysseus who he might be.

After Odysseus had recounted his story Nausicaa supplied him with clothing, fed him, gave him wine to drink and conducted him to the palace of her father. There King Alcinous and his queen, Arete, received the stranger graciously and promised to provide him with a ship to take him to his native land.

At a great feast the following night a minstrel sang of the Trojan war and of the sufferings of the returning Greeks. Alcinous saw the tears in the eyes of his visitor and quietly insisted that Odysseus tell his story.

So Odysseus told how, early in his voyage home from the war, his ship was separated from the rest of the fleet in a hurricane and how when he made landfall

it was on the coast of Libya, the land of the "wild-eyed melancholy lotus-eaters", travellers who succumbed to the narcotic dream-inducing drug of the lotus fruit. Odysseus had railed at his men, ordering them back to the ship, and sailed for Sicily where his wit and cunning were never so sorely needed.

This is Odysseus's own story.

In the cave of the one-eyed Cyclops

Although we were despondent, we sailed easily before the wind, no longer sure of our way home. That night we came to an off-shore island where thousands of goats ran wild through fertile but unworked pastures and wooded groves, drinking from fresh springs of sweet water. Smoke from a fire drifted across the narrow straits from a nearby island, but there was no sign there of ship or sailor. So, leaving the bulk of my crew on the island of goats, I crossed with twelve of my men to the mainland, taking with me a wallet of food and a flagon of strong wine.

Little did I know that we had come to the land of the Cyclopes, a fearsome race of giants whose one eye gleams horrifically from the middle of their foreheads, who feast on human flesh and who dwell in isolated caves, each family to its own territory. The leader and the most ferocious of this dreadful race was called Polyphemus, son of the sea-god Poseidon and a nymph called Thoösa.

In earlier more peaceful times Polyphemus and the Cyclopes had forged thunderbolts for Zeus under the direction of the smith god Hephaestus. But Polyphemus grew tired of being a blacksmith and encouraged his followers to abandon their trade and live by plunder and murder. He now lived alone in a dark cave devouring sheep and cattle and human kind.

It was his cave that I and my men now discovered—a cave piled high with bones and in which were penned some lambs and young goats. The sailors fell upon the goats and built up a fire on which to roast the flesh, for fresh meat was a luxury that they had long been without. While they were gathered around the spit a shadow fell across the entrance to the cave, then the light was entirely blocked out as the bulk of Polyphemus filled the doorway. After driving in his flock of sheep he rolled a great rock, heavier than twenty men could move, across the mouth of the cave. His one eye glinted in the firelight as he milked his ewes and prepared his supper. My men and I retreated further into the cave.

When at last he became aware of the men hiding in the shadows he called out in his awful voice: "Who are you, from whence do you come, and what do you want of me?"

54

"We are strangers and travellers who have lost our way," I replied courteously, "and we crave hospitality in the name of Zeus."

"What do I care for Zeus or the gods? I am mightier than they."

With that the monster reached out his great arms and snatched up two of the sailors. He dashed out their brains against the rocky floor, tore them into pieces and devoured them, flesh and bones, washing down his gruesome meal with great gulps of milk. Then he laid down and went to sleep, leaving me and my men huddled, terrified, at the rear of the cave.

With fear in my heart I roused myself and tried to move the stone that sealed the cave. I thought of my sword, but realised that even if I managed to slay the monster I and my men would be trapped in the cave by his enormous bulk. So the night of terror passed.

Early the next morning the Cyclops killed and ate two more Ithacans for breakfast, gulping more milk from a pail. After rolling away the stone he herded his flock through the entrance to the cave, then resealed it as easily as though the stone were a pebble, calling out: "Tonight I will be back for my supper!"

I knew that there must be some way to outwit this monster and already a plan was growing in my mind. By the fire was a sapling of olive wood as long as a ship's mast but still pliable. I instructed my men to cut a six-foot-long shaft and to sharpen its end to a spearpoint, which I hardened in the embers of the fire. I then hid the weapon behind a pile of goat skins.

That night Polyphemus returned and repeated his grizzly ritual: sealing up the cave, milking his herd, slaughtering and eating two more sailors.

It was now that I spoke up: "Such a meal deserves better than milk. Here is some excellent wine in a flagon. Drink it, with my compliments."

The Cyclops, who had never before tasted wine, smacked his lips. "I'll have more of that," he announced, already slurring his words.

"Indeed you shall," I retorted. "Drink your fill." Three times I filled the giant's cup with the dark, fragrant but potent wine. Three times, the fool drained the cup to the last drop.

"What is your name, stranger?" demanded Polyphemus as the wine dulled his brain and filled him with a false well-being.

"My name is No Man," I told him.

"Well then, No Man. I shall give you a present in return for the wine. You shall be the last to be eaten." Even as he spoke the Cyclops slid to the ground and fell into a drunken sleep.

I gestured to my helpers — four of whom had been drawn by lot during the day. We took the stake from its hiding place and heated its point in the fire until it gleamed as red as the Cyclops' eye. Into that eye I and my four men drove the stake, causing the giant to roar and writhe with pain and rage until the cavern echoed with his cries and the earth shook. With a mighty effort the Cyclops pulled the stake from his eye and staggered to the entrance of the cave. Rolling back the stone he bellowed across the night to his Cyclopes neighbours. They came rushing to the mouth of the cave.

"What's wrong?" they called as they gathered outside the cave. "Are you being robbed? Is someone trying to kill you? Why do you call?"

"No Man is hurting me. No Man is trying to kill me," the Cyclops roared.

"Then if no.man is hurting you, you must be 'having nightmares'. Let us be, and go back to sleep," called the giants as they dispersed and went back to their caves. "Say your prayers to your father, Poseidon."

Polyphemus roared in anger and crouched across the entrance to the cave, determined that not one of my men would escape.

What a fool he must have thought me! I racked my brain and came up with a plan. Quickly I tied three of the giant's sheep together, side by side, and fastened a man under the belly of the middle of the three. I clung to the underbelly of the largest ram of the flock, curling myself into a ball and taking firm hold of the shaggy fleece.

As the morning sunlight filtered through the entrance to the cave the herd clamoured toward the pastures. When they came to the doorway Polyphemus ran his hands over their backs and down their sides but failed to reach the men tied under the middle animal. Last of all I passed safely out of the cavern, even as the Cyclops ran his hand across the sheep's back muttering: "Ram of mine, you who are always the first out, today are the last. Are you sorrowing for your master whom No Man has befuddled with wine, blinded and out-smarted? Ah! If only I could lay hold of No Man and beat him to death I would feel better in spite of my suffering."

Free of the cave at last I could not resist taunting the Cyclops. I made my way to the beach and gained the safety of my ship. Driving the giant's herd on board I lifted anchor and put out to sea. Then I called: "Ho there Polyphemus. This is punishment from Zeus for refusing hospitality to travellers. If you are asked who it was that blinded and tricked you, it was Odysseus of Ithaca, son of Laertes!"

"So it was once foretold by a soothsayer," boomed the voice of the giant, "but I thought it would be a mighty hero of great strength, not a puny weakling such as you who tricked me with strong drink." Polyphemus lifted his arms in prayer: "Lord Poseidon, god of the deep and the mighty sea! If I am your son indeed, may Odysseus, son of Laertes, never see his home again! Or should he ever reach home, may it be only after long, exhausting years, hardship and trouble. May he lose his ship's company, and may he find only trouble and confusion at home!"

With that imprecation the Cyclops tore at the hillside and broke away a mighty boulder which he hurled seaward in the direction of my taunts. It fell

astern of the ship causing a mighty wave to carry the vessel forward to where the remainder of the fleet and my sailors were awaiting the return of their companions. With heavy hearts we left the island, joyful at our escape but grieving for the dear friends we had left.

Poseidon had indeed heard the prayer of his terrible and unfortunate son, and it was many a weary year before Odysseus saw the rocky shores of Ithaca again where trouble lay coiled like a serpent waiting to strike from the shadows.

The unfolding of the Odyssey

Many were the trials of Odysseus as he sailed toward his homeland, Ithaca. At the island of Aeolus, the lord of the winds gathered into a goatskin all the winds except the one which was to blow the adventurer home. But his men were impatient and greedy and unloosed the bag while their master slept, thinking that it contained treasure. The winds rushed out and blew the ship back along its course to Aeolus, who refused to help Odysseus again.

On the island ruled by the goddess Circe, the enchantress turned Odysseus's men into swine and only when Hermes gave Odysseus a counter-charm could he outwit Circe. Even so Odysseus could not finally leave until he had made a terrible journey to the Kingdom of the Dead. Then he had to pass the island of the Sirens, who lured sailors to destruction by their singing. So Odysseus blocked the ears of his men with wax and lashed himself to the mast. After that he sailed between Scylla and Charybdis — Scylla, a fearsome monster with twelve legs and six long monstrous necks, and Charybdis, the whirlpool which sucked down water three times a day and then spewed it back again.

When at last he reached Ithaca he was alone, his men having all been drowned or destroyed. He woke on his first morning in his homeland to find the goddess Athena, his protector, by his side. Telemachus, his son, had gone to Sparta to try to gain news of his father, she told him. Moreover, his wife Penelope had been beseiged by suitors who believed that Odysseus was dead, but she had kept them at bay by promising that she would choose one of them when she completed a shroud which she was weaving for Laertes, Odysseus's father. She worked on it all day, said Athena, and at night she unravelled what she had completed. When Odysseus showed signs of rushing to his wife's aid Athena advised him to be wary: he had changed greatly and could he be certain that his wife wouldn't see in him yet another stranger?

So Odysseus allowed Athena to turn him into a gnarled, bent old man who shambled forward with shuffling gait. The goddess took him to a hut owned by a shepherd who had worked for Odysseus before he sailed for Troy. At the same time she summoned Telemachus back from Sparta.

Three nights later, as Odysseus in his beggar's guise sat by the fire talking over the past with his old shepherd friend, the door creaked open and Telemachus entered the hut. Sadly he approached the old shepherd and began to tell of his fruitless search for his beloved father, while Odysseus listened to his son's story.

"Go now to my mother," said Telemachus to the shepherd. "Tell her that I am here again but dare not come to her openly, for her suitors want my blood."

When the shepherd left to do the bidding of Telemachus, Athena appeared before Odysseus and told him it was time to reveal himself to his son. As she spoke she touched him with her golden wand. At the touch his strength and youthful vigour were restored, his skin grew tanned once more, his hair darkened and a clean mantle and tunic were hung from his shoulders. Telemachus looked at this with amazement.

"Surely you must be one of the Immortals!" he declared.

"Not so. I am no god; but I *am* your father," Odysseus replied.

When Telemachus had heard his story he flung his arms around his noble father and the tears coursed down his cheek. Long into the night they talked and when dawn came Odysseus promised his son that together they would outwit the suitors who wanted the death of Telemachus and the hand of Penelope.

Once more in his disguise as a beggar, Odysseus approached the palace, having sent Telemachus ahead. Arriving at the palace gates he stopped and gazed wistfully at his home. Lying before the gate was an ancient hunting dog, covered with sores and wheezing in the shade. But its tail thumped a greeting, for this was Argos, his favourite dog of years before.

Inside the palace the suitors, gorging themselves with roast meat and red wine, taunted and mocked Odysseus and would have flung him out had not Telemachus placed himself in front of his father and defended him. Hearing what was happening, Penelope herself summoned the beggar into her presence and courteously welcomed him to her hearth.

Sensing a tenderness in the stranger she told him of her sadness over her husband's absence and her problems with the suitors. She confided in him a plan she had formed.

"Tomorrow I intend to bring out the great bow which only Odysseus could string. I am going to line up twelve axes with ceremonial rings in the hall. Whoever of my suitors can string the bow and shoot an arrow through the rings I will marry."

"Perhaps I shall try myself," murmured the old beggar.

"Perhaps you shall," replied Penelope softly. "In the meantime I shall call my old nurse to bathe your feet and look to your needs. So sleep well until the morrow."

On the morrow, which was Apollo's feast day, it happened as Penelope had decreed. Twelve axes were set up and the great bow was brought out. One by one the suitors tried to string the bow, only to be defeated. Odysseus sat in the shadows watching. At last he stepped forward to claim his turn. The hall buzzed with anger. Telemachus spoke up on the beggar's behalf and Penelope gently bade him try his hand.

Swiftly he pulled a long, slender arrow from a quiver at his feet, fitted it perfectly to the strung bow and took aim. The arrow winged its way surely through the rings to embed itself in the wall beyond. Again his disguise fell away and Odysseus in all his heroic manhood stood before the company.

The suitors in their frustration turned upon Odysseus and would have killed him, but Telemachus sprang to his side and together father and son fought side by side until over a hundred corpses littered the hall. The hall was scrubbed clean and, at last, Penelope approached the hero. Telemachus withdrew and husband and wife embraced one another alone. Even then Penelope dared not believe that it was Odysseus returned. Only when Odysseus whispered to her the secret of the complicated making of the bed of olive wood which they had shared together so long ago did Penelope know for sure that this was her husband, returned as though from the dead. Penelope rose again and embraced her husband. Home was the hero, his long odyssey completed!

In years to come Odysseus was to tell the story of his wanderings many times over. Serenity came to him in old age, but only after he had made his peace with Poseidon. Carrying an oar on his shoulder he journeyed through the mainland until he met a man who lived so far from the sea that he thought the oar was a winnowing fan, used to separate chaff from wheat. It was here that he founded a shrine to the sea-god.

He returned home and reigned peacefully until at last he fulfilled the prophecy of Tiresias, the blind seer of Thebes: "Death will come to you in its gentlest guise from the sea. When he takes you, you will be worn out after an easy old age, and surrounded by prosperous people."

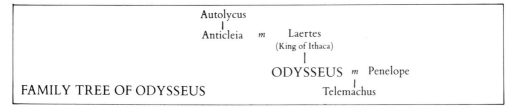

Autolycus
|
Anticleia   *m*   Laertes
(King of Ithaca)
|
ODYSSEUS   *m*   Penelope
|
FAMILY TREE OF ODYSSEUS   Telemachus

Sumeria and Babylon

One of the world's greatest early civilisations developed about 4000 B.C. in the plain of Shinar between the Tigris and the Euphrates rivers. The area was called Sumeria and Babylon was one of its ancient cities. The people were generally known as Sumerians and, later, Babylonians. They were farmers and traders. Trade and government provided the need for records, which the Sumerians scratched as primitive pictures with the tip of a reed on a flat, oval disk of soft clay later hardened by the sun or baked in an oven. From these pictures developed the 560 or more signs and phonetic symbols of Sumerian writing.

Each Sumerian town had its own temple, surrounded by a massive wall. The temple was a place of worship, a storehouse and the centre of business. The temple property was in the care of the priests and scribes who supervised the building of the tower-temple as a sanctuary to Enlil, the Sumerian god of the air.

City kingdoms developed about 3000 B.C., the most important being Ur. About 2500 B.C. a Semitic chieftain called Sargon made himself lord of all the plain of Shinar and adopted the Sumerian civilisation. Gradually there developed a literature rich in story to answer the questions of life and death and the nature of man. There were religious myths to explain the creation of the world, stories of how the gods taught human beings the arts and crafts of civilisation. There were stories about the mighty deeds of kings and legends of both kings and heroes.

These included the wonderful adventures of a shepherd called Etana who, when his flocks became diseased, mounted the back of an eagle and flew off in search of the herb which was the source of life. Although he was hurled to the earth, this is possibly the oldest story of man's attempt to fly.

There was another hero called Adapa who was a fisherman. When his boat was overturned by the wind-goddess, Adapa became so angry that he broke her wing. He was then summoned before the sky-god who eventually offered Adapa the bread and water of life, but he refused it and so lost the possibility of eternal life for himself and all mankind. Another hero and his wife survived a great flood in the manner of Noah in the Old Testament.

But the greatest hero of the Sumerians was Gilgamesh, said to be the Sumerian ancestor of Heracles. There still exists an early Babylonian cylinder seal showing in the centre Gilgamesh slaying a wild bull. On the left- and right-hand panels, Enkidu, the friend of Gilgamesh, wrestles with a lion.

Gilgamesh: The Epic Hero of the Sumerians

This oldest surviving epic poem in the world was probably being told or sung, accompanied by the harp, three thousand years before Christ was born. It was written down in cuneiform letters on clay tablets in the second millennium B.C., at least five hundred years before the *Iliad* and the *Odyssey* were written down. The Babylonians took the stories of Gilgamesh, perhaps the first tragic hero in literature, from the Sumerians who were the first inhabitants of Mesopotamia to develop writing. Tablets of the poems were preserved in the library of Assurbanipal, the last great king of Assyria.

The tablets were lost and the poems forgotten until fragments were excavated about the middle of the nineteenth century. Over the years more and more tablets have been unearthed and scholars have been able to piece together one of the world's most ancient stories, which tells not only of the wondrous exploits of Gilgamesh, the powerful king of Uruk, but also of his deep affection for his friend, Enkidu. Like the friendship of David and Jonathan in the Bible, the relationship between Gilgamesh and Enkidu outlasted quarrels, and the names of the two heroes will always go hand in hand.

Gilgamesh, this most ancient of heroes, was not only given to mighty deeds but he was a dreamer who searched for knowledge and the meaning of life. He was part god and part man. From his divine mother Ninsun he inherited beauty of form. Shamash the sun-god perfected his beauty and he was given the strength of a bull, as well as a strange restlessness. From his high-priest father he inherited mortality.

Unlike many heroes of other cultures the birth of Gilgamesh was unremarkable, and we know nothing of his childhood. We meet him first as a proud, tyrannical ruler from whom no woman, young or old, is safe and whose arrogance stirred the citizens of Uruk to complain to the gods about his behaviour . . .

The creation of Enkidu

When Anu, the great god of Uruk, heard the cries of the other gods about the overbearing Gilgamesh, he summoned the earth-goddess Aruru to his presence. "You are the goddess of creation and responsible for the birth of Gilgamesh. Now create a man his equal in strength and restlessness who will rival him in his feats of strength and who will lead him to far adventures."

Aruru dipped her hand in water and moulded clay into the shape of a man and let it fall into the wilderness, where it received the breath of life and was called Enkidu. This man-creature was rough and his body was matted and covered with long hair which tumbled about his shoulders like a woman's. He didn't know that he was a man but ran with the gazelles and other beasts, eating grass and drinking with them at waterholes.

A hunter who caught sight of Enkidu filling up the pits he had dug, tearing his traps apart and helping wild beasts escape was numbed with terror, for he believed this man-creature to be the strongest in the world. The trapper went to his father in fear and told him what he had seen. The old man in his wisdom told his son to go to Gilgamesh, who was as strong as a star from the heavens and against whom no man was a match, and to ask his help in catching this wild creature.

When Gilgamesh heard the story he laughed and said, "He can be tamed only by a beautiful woman. Take one into the wilderness with you and when Enkidu sees her beauty and is filled with desire for her he will become like other men."

So the hunter took a young girl of great beauty with him; and as Enkidu came with the gazelles to the watering place at evening the girl showed herself openly to the savage, who saw her and forgot everything but her beauty. The girl stayed with the wild man for six days and seven nights and when Enkidu returned to his animal friends they ran away from him, fleeing in terror because, to them, he was now like any other man.

Enkidu realised what had happened and returned to the girl who had won him and said, "I am no longer brother to the gazelles and the wild things. Take me to where you live with other human beings."

"I will take you to strong-walled Uruk where lives Gilgamesh the mighty who is like a wild bull among men and of whom there is no equal on earth," she replied.

"Take me, woman, to this man and I will challenge him boldly. I will call out: 'I am the strongest of the strong for was I not born in the hills and did I not run with the animals of the wilderness? Come and wrestle with me if you dare.'" So spoke Enkidu.

Then the girl took part of her clothing to cover the wild man and she led him to the tents of shepherds, who crowded around to see this savage that had been tamed. They offered him bread but he couldn't eat it, having only ever sucked the milk of wild animals. The girl had to teach him to eat and drink as other men.

After seven goblets of wine he smoothed down the matted hair of his body and put on clothing like other men. He went hunting and caught lions and wolves so that the herdsmen could rest peacefully.

Enkidu would have been happy living with the shepherds but the girl urged him to return with her to Uruk and challenge the king, Gilgamesh. As the two of them entered the market-place of Uruk, people pushed and jostled to gaze on Enkidu.

"He is the image of Gilgamesh."

"No, he is shorter."

"But he is bigger boned."

"Look, he is stronger than Gilgamesh. He was reared on the milk of wild beasts."

"Gilgamesh will meet his match with this one."

"He has the looks of a god, a hero. He must be greater than Gilgamesh."

Even while they were speaking Gilgamesh himself approached with a roll of drums, and the two met at the gate of a house which Gilgamesh was about to enter. Looking directly at the ruler Enkidu put out his foot and blocked his entry. Insulted and enraged Gilgamesh took hold of his opponent to fling him aside.

So they grappled at one another like wild bulls wrestling for command of the herd. The earth shook, they broke the doorposts and the walls began to buckle; they heaved and they snorted with fury. For a time the odds seemed even until Gilgamesh was able to bend his knee with his foot planted firmly on the ground, and he threw Enkidu to the earth.

Immediately hate no longer flooded the heart of Gilgamesh. Instead it was filled with love.

And so it was with Enkidu. Looking up from the dust he said, "There is no other like you in the world. Your strength is like that of an ox in the field and a lion in the forest. It surpasses that of any man." So saying he rose and embraced Gilgamesh. Their friendship was sealed from that day onward and they became closer than brothers.

Adventures in the forest

Gilgamesh and his friend Enkidu sat together as kings in Uruk, both royally robed and wearing golden crowns. They were honoured equally by the citizens and the nobles of Uruk.

But Gilgamesh was restless still, and strange dreams troubled him as he slept. Enkidu tried to comfort him: "Do not be depressed. Everlasting life may not be your destiny, but kingship is. Rule wisely and well." Even as he spoke Enkidu himself felt downcast and he sighed deeply and admitted to his friend, "I myself, Gilgamesh, desire action. I am oppressed by idleness."

It was then that Gilgamesh resolved to go on a journey to the Country of the Living where, in the great Forest of Cedars, lived a ferocious giant called Humbaba. To Enkidu he confided: "I have not yet had my name engraved on bricks of clay; my destiny is not fulfilled. You and I must go together to the forest and fight the evil that lives there."

"When I lived with the beasts," replied Enkidu, "I came upon that forest of which you speak. It is ten thousand leagues long, and as broad; and it is guarded by the devilish Humbaba whose roar is louder than any storm, whose breath is fiery, whose jaws are death to any man. He guards the forest so well that the forest animals sixty leagues away hear him when he stirs. What's more, he never sleeps and is on guard day and night. How could we overpower such a guardian?"

"I know that only the gods are immortal," replied Gilgamesh. "But if I fall in the fight against evil, my name will endure forever. So let me lead the way and let us go forward together that we may be remembered together."

"First go to Shamash, the sun-god, for the land where the cedar grows is his. Beg his advice," implored Enkidu.

So Gilgamesh took two kids, a brown one and one pure white; he held them to his breast and carried them into the presence of Shamash. He raised his silver sceptre and called: "Hear me, O Shamash, hear me. I go to the Forest of Cedars, the land of Humbaba, so that my name may be among the famous. Grant me strength and succour. If I die in that land I shall not mind, but if I return I will raise a glorious monument to the gods and praise you forever."

Shamash accepted the entreaties of Gilgamesh and he appointed strong men as allies for Gilgamesh, stationing them in mountain caves; and he instructed the great winds of the earth to help him.

Gilgamesh was glad in his heart and he ordered armourers to forge weapons for himself and Enkidu: axes, swords and bows — the heaviest in the world. His own axe he called "Strength of Heroes". Then he strode into the market-place of

Uruk and spoke to the people: "I, Gilgamesh, your ruler, go now to the Forest of Cedars to kill the evil monster, Humbaba. All the world shall hear of this enterprise and my name shall live forever."

No matter how hard his counsellors tried to dissuade him, Gilgamesh stood firm, but before they set out he took Enkidu by the hand to visit his mother the great Queen Ninsun, and asked her to pray to Shamash on their behalf.

So Ninsun clothed herself in a sweeping gown, placed her tiara on her head and climbed to the palace roof where stood the great altar of the sun. There she burnt incense and raised her arms in prayer as the smoke ascended to Shamash himself.

Having blessed Gilgamesh she called Enkidu and said: "Although you are not the child of my body I call you my adopted son. You are my other child; serve your brother well." Then as she placed an amulet around his neck she said: "I am entrusting my son to your care. Bring him back safely to me."

Then the counsellors also blessed the young men and warned Gilgamesh not to be rash. "Let Enkidu walk in front. He knows the ways of the forest and he has seen Humbaba; let him watch for you and protect you."

"Forward then," called Enkidu. "I know the way of the forest and its evil guardian. There is nothing to fear, I tell you."

With these words the two friends departed and walked fifty leagues in one day. In three days they had crossed seven mountains and came to the door of the forest. They entered the forest together and walked to the foot of the green mountain where great cedar trees towered upward to heaven—the dwelling place of the gods and where stands the throne of Ishtar the great goddess. There Gilgamesh dug a well and prayed for a sign as he lay down to sleep.

At midnight he shook Enkidu. "I have had the most terrible dream. I was in the wilderness fighting a wild bull which bellowed and bit at my arm. Then I fell forward and found that someone was bathing me with water from a water-skin."

Enkidu said, "You have no cause to fear. The wild bull is our protector Shamash who will take you by the arm in your hour of peril. The one who gave you water is your family god. With his aid and my support you shall accomplish your mission and your name will live forever."

The next day the friends travelled another fifty leagues before pitching their camp. Both Enkidu and Gilgamesh dreamed terrible dreams that night. The next morning as they descended the mountain slope Gilgamesh seized his axe and began to fell one of the huge cedar trees.

Far away Humbaba heard the noise and broke into a fury. "Who is trespassing in my forest and cutting down my cedars?" he roared.

Gilgamesh stopped in his place, held as though in a profound sleep. "Do not be afraid. Keep going," called Shamash from heaven. So Gilgamesh roused himself and buckled on his breastplate, "The Voice of Heroes", and strode forward.

Enkidu had more to fear. The memory of Humbaba rose before him and he was terrified. Gilgamesh felt his companion's fear and called: "Throw away fear. Take up your axe and attack. You will never know peace if you leave the fight unfinished."

"Forward," shouted Enkidu as Humbaba came into view snuffling and pawing the ground, shaking his enormous head and menacing Gilgamesh with his wild and ferocious eye—the eye of death.

"Help me, Shamash!" cried Gilgamesh, clutching the hilt of his sword.

Great Shamash heard his prayer and called up the winds of the earth: the wind from the north, the whirlwind, the wind of storm, ice and tempest, the searing, scorching wind of the desert. They came like a fire-storm, like forked lightning and a mountain deluge. The winds beat upon Humbaba until he stood rooted like a tree, unable to go forward or retreat.

Gilgamesh wielded his axe like a scythe. He felled seven cedar trees in seven blows, bound them into bundles and used them to scale the mountain till he reached the monster's lair.

Humbaba still stood buffeted and bound by the winds. His eyes filled with tears and he begged for mercy. "I was born of the mountain and made keeper of the forest. Free me and I shall be your servant forever."

Moved by this plea Gilgamesh turned to Enkidu: "Should not the snared bird return to its nest and the bound man be restored to his mother's arms?"

"If that be allowed, my friend, then be sure that you will never return to the city where your mother awaits you. The monster will betray you and bar your way."

Gilgamesh knew that Enkidu spoke truth. He drew his sword from his belt and thrust at the monster's neck. Enkidu struck the second blow and at the third Humbaba was felled like one of the cedars of the forest.

As far away as two leagues the trees of the forest trembled and shook. The mountains and the hills shivered, for the guardian of the forest was dead.

Gilgamesh and Enkidu together cleared a great swathe through the forest to the banks of the Euphrates. They kissed the ground and offered the head of Humbaba to Enlil, the god who ruled over air and earth. They cleaned their weapons and bathed long in the river until they were clean again. They changed into fresh, new clothing. Gilgamesh arrayed himself in the robes of royalty and placed his crown upon his head. His heart was filled with peace and joy, for he believed that he had fulfilled his destiny with the help of his friend, Enkidu.

When the goddess Ishtar saw Gilgamesh in his royal splendour she fell in love with him and, in a forest glade, appeared before him in her divine beauty, but as a woman. "Marry me, Gilgamesh, and you shall have a golden chariot decorated with lapis lazuli, drawn by demons of the storm instead of horses."

Much more did Ishtar promise Gilgamesh, but he was not moved by the false promises of the goddess, knowing full well that any man who had ever succumbed to her wiles had been turned into a bird or a beast, or had been killed.

Ishtar flew into a whirlwind of rage and, in revenge against Gilgamesh, she led the Bull of Heaven to Uruk and set it free. When Gilgamesh and Enkidu reached Uruk the bull caused the ground to crack open with its snorting and raging. A hundred men fell to their death. The bull snorted again, and two hundred fell through the fissures in the earth.

At the third snort Enkidu leapt at the bull and seized it by the horns, calling to Gilgamesh: "We boasted that we would leave famous names behind us. Now thrust your sword between the neck and the horns." Gilgamesh seized the bull by the tail and stabbed as Enkidu directed. Then they cut out the heart of the bull and offered it as a sacrifice to Shamash. After that the brothers rested.

Ishtar knew then that she had no power over Gilgamesh, but her anger was now unbounded and she determined to have her revenge. From the tower she cursed Gilgamesh and Enkidu.

But Enkidu tossed the bull's right thigh into her face, and it hangs in the sky to this day. Gilgamesh called the smiths and armourers and commanded them to coat the horns of the bull with lapis lazuli two fingers thick and to hang them on the wall of the city. The heroes then washed their hands in the Euphrates and drove through the streets of the city in celebration.

But that night Enkidu knew in his dreams that Ishtar's curse had fallen on him and that he was dying. Ten days he lay on his bed, and each day his suffering increased. The lamentations of Gilgamesh were of no avail. On the twelfth day he called to his friend and said: "The great goddess has cursed me and I must die in shame for I shall not fall in battle like heroes do."

Gilgamesh wept over the body of his friend and at dawn his voice rose in mourning. He voiced an elegy for his companion. Then when he knew that his friend was really dead he raged like a lion, tore his hair and flung down his robes. For seven days and seven nights he wept. Then he ordered the coppersmiths, goldsmiths and stonemasons to fashion a giant statue of his friend. When it was finished he ordered a table to be set up before it. On it was placed a bowl of carnelian filled with honey and a bowl of lapis lazuli filled with butter. These Gilgamesh uncovered and offered to the sun in memory of Enkidu; then, weeping bitterly, he walked away.

After that Gilgamesh himself was plagued with the fear of death. He determined to leave home and go in search of everlasting life. He survived many dangers and arrived at last at the garden of Siduri, the "Woman of the Vine" at the rim of the ocean. She directed him to Urshanabi, the ferryman, who would punt him over the waters of death to Utnashapishtim, called the Faraway, who lived at Dilmun where the sun goes down and to whom the gods had given the gift of eternal life.

But Utnashapishtim for all his experience could not help Gilgamesh in his quest. "All men must die," he told the hero. "On earth there is no such thing as forever. We do not build a house to last forever and no contract is permanently sealed. The sleeping and the dead are alike, for sleeping is but the image of death. The gods allot life and death, but the day of his death is disclosed to no man."

Utnashapishtim could do no more except that he told Gilgamesh of a magic plant that grew at the bottom of the sea which, if it is eaten, brings back a man's lost youth. Gilgamesh ordered Urshanabi to row him to where the plant grew. He tied heavy stones to his feet and sank to the sea-bed where he braved the thorns and plucked the plant. When he tore the stones from his feet he shot back to the surface clutching his precious plant.

On his way home Gilgamesh made a camp by a well of clear water. While he was swimming a serpent snatched his plant, sloughed its skin and returned to the well. The serpent but not Gilgamesh had become young again.

Gilgamesh wept bitterly and lamented: "Was it for this that I laboured and spent my life's blood? I have gained nothing. But before I die I shall engrave my name on the walls of Uruk."

So Gilgamesh's search for everlasting life was in vain, for he died as all men must one day die. As for the hero, his name lives on — not only engraved in stone but immortalised in story and song.

Old Scandinavia

From Norse mythology we have our English days of the week. Tuesday, Wednesday, Thursday and Friday are named after the old Norse gods of whom Odin (Woden in Old English) was the supreme ruler.

Odin was the god of battle and death. Two black ravens perched on his shoulders. Each morning they flew off in opposite directions and returned each evening after having circled the world to report back to Odin. Two great wolves, symbols of power, sat at Odin's feet. He owned an immense eight-legged horse called Sleipnir. Odin had obtained the secret of the Runes, which were letters with magic properties, so that he mastered not only the art of writing but also of magic.

Frigg, the wife of Odin, shared his throne and her ear was always ready to hear the prayers of women. Thor was the strongest of the Norse gods and he possessed three magical weapons: a hammer, an iron glove and a belt of power. Loki, of the nimble mind and smooth tongue, was originally a frost giant and could change his shape at will.

The Norse world was divided into a number of regions. The earth where mortals lived was surrounded by Midgard. Below the earth was a land called Darkalfheim where dwarfs or gnomes mined for precious metals. But there was also a sunny place called Alfheim where the elves lived. Then there was Asgard where the gods lived and which abounded in gold and silver. Asgard was guarded by a huge wall and rainbow bridge called Bifrost.

Valhalla was Odin's hall of slain heroes. Norse nobles who fell bravely in battle were brought to Valhalla by the Valkyries, maidens who were daughters of the gods. Any warrior who felt their touch knew he was doomed to die; but if he were particularly brave Odin himself offered him his portion of warrior's mead in Valhalla. From then on the warrior would live, eat, drink and fight in this world of supreme heroes.

In old Norse or Viking mythology, as in the Greek, there were gods, demi-gods and heroes. One of the greatest heroes was Sigurd — known in Germanic legend as Siegfried, the central character of Wagner's four great musical dramas, *The Ring of the Nibelungs*.

The Volsungs were a race particularly favoured by Odin, from whom they were descended. Sigi, the founder of the line, overcame great difficulties to acquire his kingdom; he was even regarded as one of Odin's sons, giving Sigurd a divine ancestry.

The *Eddas*, or ancient Icelandic poems, together with the prose saga of the Volsungs are part of the Norse mythology passed down to the Scandinavians, the British and the Germans. In the second half of the ninth century A.D., Norwegians, fleeing from the bondage of King Harald, sailed to Iceland and later to Greenland. Some settled along the way in England, Scotland and Ireland. They took with them the songs or *Eddas* dating from as early as the seventh century. Further songs were composed and sung during the tenth and eleventh centuries: all these became a mixture of Norse, Celtic, German and Anglo-Saxon legends.

The collected *Edda* contains tales of gods and heroes. The so-called *Elder Edda* has been referred to as the *Iliad* of the North. Norsemen in the Middle Ages looked back to Sigmund and Sigurd just as the Greeks looked back to their great heroes. The *Elder Edda* belonged, of course, to an oral tradition, but the songs were at some time written down on vellum sheets which were discovered in an Icelandic farmhouse in the seventeenth century.

The *Younger Edda* — the *Prose Edda* — is a textbook for poets and was written partly by Snorri Sturlson, a famous literary figure in Iceland, who lived between about 1179 and 1241. It contains something of the Volsung story.

About five hundred years later an unknown Icelandic author wrote the *Volsunga Saga*, a prose telling of the Volsung poems in the *Elder Edda*. This thirteenth century Icelandic story was translated into English and later put into verse form by William Morris, the famous founder of the Kelmscott Press, in 1876.

So, like most myths and legends, there is more than one source of the old Scandinavian epics as we have them today.

Sigurd of the Volsungs

The Volsungs were a royal family whose exploits are recorded in the old Norse *Volsunga Saga*. Volsung had nine sons, the youngest of whom was Sigmund.

At the wedding feast of Sigmund's twin sister, Signy, a poor-looking, one-eyed stranger appeared carrying in his right hand a naked sword whose splendour outshone the sun. Now the great hall in which the wedding feast was being celebrated had been built around the vast girth of a living oak tree known throughout the land as Branstock. All eyes followed the silent stranger, who strode through the crowd directly to the trunk of Branstock. Raising the sword high in the air he struck forward burying the bright blade up to its glittering jewelled hilt in the massive tree-trunk.

"The sword belongs to whoever is able to pluck it from the tree. There is no finer sword in the world." So saying, the stranger, who was Odin in disguise, bowed and departed.

A murmur of anticipation ran through the Vikings there present. First, Siggeir, the great lord of the Goths who had come to marry Signy, approached the tree. Grasping the jewelled hilt of the sword he strained to draw it from the wood, but it moved not a whit. Shamefaced and with an angry heart, Siggeir made his way back to the high-seat, determined that one day the sword would be his.

Then the earls of Siggeir took their turn, but for all their muscular strength the sword of Odin moved not an inch from its resting place.

One by one the Vikings stepped forward. King Volsung and each of his sons tried in vain until the youngest, Sigmund, stepped up to the tree. Grasping the magnificent hilt the young man slid the blade from the trunk as if through smooth oil.

Deep in his heart Siggeir vowed that he would gain possession of the sword of the Branstock—Odin's sword. He returned to his home in Gothland where he plotted the downfall of the Volsungs. His scheme was to invite King Volsung and his court to visit Gothland, planning to ambush the Volsungs as they came ashore from their longships.

Some time later the Volsungs, unaware of Siggeir's plan, landed on the coast of Gothland. It was with great surprise that they found the shoreline brimming with spear-wielding Goths. During the battle that ensued the Volsungs, unprepared and outnumbered, fared badly. At the beginning of the conflict King Volsung fell mortally wounded. His sons, amidst the sad sight of their fallen comrades, were captured, bound and left in the woods to die. But it wasn't until Sigmund's sword was taken from him that Siggeir's heart was glad. The sword of Odin was his at last.

Still not satisfied Siggeir vowed the death of the Volsungs. But Signy, Sigmund's sister and Siggeir's wife, begged her husband not to kill them. Instead they were tethered in the wildwood, from where Signy secretly planned to help them escape.

So the sons of King Volsung were bound to trees and left there as prey for the wild beasts that roamed the forest. Before Signy could send them aid all but Sigmund and Sigi were devoured. When Siggeir's woodmen next reported to him they brought the news that there was no one left on the tree-beam. Only the bones and cords remained, they said.

Hearing this report Signy grew as white as death. Thrusting her maid-servants aside she fled her bower and made her way to the wildwood, where darkness had fallen. At last she came to the tree where Sigmund was bound. There in the moonlight stood a mighty man, his clothing torn and bloody, his face gaunt and his eyes weary and hollow. It was Sigmund who, after Sigi had succumbed to the attacking wolves, had fought them off with his teeth, and survived. Clasping her brother to her breast Signy promised to help him if he would but hide in the wildwood and make himself a lair.

For many years Sigmund lived in secret, supported by the gifts his sister sent him. She even sent her son, Sinfiotli, to be fostered by her brother in his woodland hideaway. For three years they lived together before Sigmund told the lad of Siggeir's treachery. Together they bided the time when Sigmund would take his revenge.

When winter came and the nights had grown long, the two men stole through the forest to Siggeir's dwelling. There they hid themselves behind wine-casks in a chamber close to the feast-hall. But they were discovered when a toy, which belonged to Signy's younger children, rolled behind the casks. The two men drew their swords and fought desperately until Siggeir's earls overpowered them by weight of numbers. At Siggeir's command the two were imprisoned in adjoining chambers in a stone fortress.

Signy's grief was great, but she was resolute in her determination to help her brother and her son. So she bribed the guards with gold and threw a parcel wrapped in straw into Sinfiotli's cell. The guards thought it was food, but in the parcel was the sword of Odin which Signy had stolen from her husband.

Sinfiotli called his discovery to Sigmund through the stone which divided their cells. It wasn't long before Sigmund heard a grinding sound at the wall. Soon the hefty blade pierced its way through the rock. Sinfiotli and Sigmund furiously used the blade as a saw until they had cut their way through. Then they hacked through the rafters of the prison and were free.

That night the two men piled fallen oak trees against the King's dwelling and set fire to them. Sigmund took up his position at the gate door and Sinfiotli by the door used by the women. As the flames took hold the men of Siggeir surged through the doorway. Sigmund cut them down one by one. At the women's doorway, Signy appeared in her royal robes. Quickly and briefly she took leave of her son. Then she turned to Sigmund.

"Now all shall know how much I loved the Volsung name. Farewell, my brother. Remember me in death. For with Siggeir I must die."

Even as she was speaking the flames encircled the King's throne. Quickly she kissed her brother, then made her way through the smoke and ruins to the King's side. At that moment the great roof-tree shuddered and snapped. The rafters collapsed. Siggeir and Signy were engulfed in flaming debris. Such was the end of one who ruled by treachery; and Signy perished at his side.

Sigmund and Sinfiotli returned to the land of the Volsungs where Sinfiotli became a great warrior. Sigmund was crowned king and married Borghild who was fair and comely.

The sword of Odin served Sigmund well in battle. But as the years passed he dwelt alone, for Borghild had gone from him and he had no heir. So he made an offer to King Eylini of the Islands for the hand of his daughter, Hiordis. She was as wise as she was lovely, and fit to be a queen of the Volsungs. But another king, Lyngi, who ruled a nearby realm and who was brave, young and fair also sought the hand of Hiordis in marriage. King Eylini knew that there would be strife when Hiordis made her choice.

Hiordis knew her mind and chose whose queen she would be. "Should I, who am called wise, choose aught but the greatest of kings? Tell Sigmund that I would be honoured to become his queen."

Sigmund lost no time in getting ready his longships. He and his earls, a goodly company, sailed for the kingdom of Eylini. The wedding of Sigmund and Hiordis was followed by a great and abundant feast.

But already Lyngi was preparing his longships to cross the sea. He was determined to claim Hiordis, come what may.

Sigmund prepared for war. Breaking the peace-strings, he drew forth the gleaming sword of Odin. In the battle that followed King Sigmund's armour shone like gold in the sun at noon, his sword flashed and his hair blew white in the wind, for he was now an old man. It was when the fighting was at its fiercest that a one-eyed stranger, wearing a black cape and a hat turned up at the side, appeared before him. The sad-looking man brandished the longest and stoutest spear that Sigmund had ever seen. Sigmund lunged forward with his trusty sword but this last time it failed him and the blade broke into three separate pieces. Sigmund knew in his heart that Odin himself had come to call him to his final resting place in Valhalla.

But before Sigmund died he entrusted the pieces of his sword to his wife, Queen Hiordis, who then escaped the scene of the battle by boat, drifting across the sea to the coast of Denmark. Hiordis was received into Denmark's royal family and in time married Alf, the king's son, who became the stepfather to her baby son fathered by Sigmund, Sigurd.

When but a boy Sigurd was apprenticed to Regin who, though a dwarf, was a famous blacksmith—an honourable and vitally important trade at a time when tempered steel and burnished shields could save a man's life and honour. Moreover Regin was versed in magic and could read and carve the ancient runic symbols. These arts he passed on to his royal apprentice. He taught him, too, to speak in many tongues, to play sweetly upon the harp and delight the hearts of his hearers with melodious songs. Sigurd grew into a skilful hunter, and he was known to kill with his bare hands wild mountain bulls and the wolves of the wood.

Although Regin was a fine teacher he was also a trouble-maker. Once, when he was speaking to Sigurd of the far-off deeds of the Volsung kings, he taunted the lad saying, "Why don't you ride in the manner of your forefathers? Go to your stepfather and demand a battle-steed worthy of your Volsung ancestry."

"I have as many horses as my heart desires," replied Sigurd. "What more do I need?"

"The very best that the land offers, that is what you need," insisted Regin. "You must be allowed to choose one of the horses of Gripir, for there are none like them." Then he struck upon the harp and filled the heart of Sigurd with battle songs, and stirred his blood with a desire for glory.

That night Sigurd approached his stepfather, King Alf, and was granted permission to visit the hall of Gripir where the old sage sat on a dais carved from the tooth of a sea-beast, wearing a gown of woven gold, and holding a regal staff the head of which was made of crystal. To Sigurd Gripir gave his blessing, and

permission to hunt in his meadow for the finest of his wild horses — a mount fit only for a king.

On his way to the meadow Sigurd was accosted by a stranger, one-eyed and very old. "Be not in such a hurry. Stay a while. I know the mountains and the countryside well and I can help you in your quest," said the Old One.

"Is it for gold that you offer help?" asked Sigurd. "Surely not. You have the shining face of the mighty men of old of whom Regin speaks."

"It is that I know the horses well, and I know you. Come, I will help you."

So the Ancient One and the youth went out and drove the horses down the mountainside and across the meadow to a rushing river of turbulent water. The two men drove the herd straight into the torrent. Many a brave steed floundered; some were caught in eddies, and some sank under the force of the water. And of those who made the farthest bank there was one fine grey stallion who tossed his mane as he galloped across the meadow, then wheeled and took the river again, breasting the water and scrambling up the bank near where Sigurd stood.

The Old One spoke to the youth: "Listen Sigurd. I once gave your father, Sigmund, a gift which will come to you one day. But this horse is my gift to you. Ride him bravely and well, wherever you go; and ride him on missions befitting a Volsung and a king!"

Then the stranger set his face to the mountain and around him shone a great light which dimmed, then disappeared, and Sigurd knew that Odin had bequeathed him a steed in whose veins ran the blood of Sleipnir, the eight-legged mount of the greatest of the gods. And Sigurd caught the horse and called him Greyfell because he was the colour of storm clouds.

The slaying of Fafnir

As the days passed Sigurd grew strong and handsome in body, noble of mind and spirit. He was loved by all, especially the children. All who knew him respected him. But he was sometimes restless within and it troubled him that he was growing up in an alien land and not among his own kin. He saw the sons of his mother and King Alf growing to maturity and he knew that he would be true to them always; but he would not be their servant.

Regin recognised the restlessness within the youth and he often spoke with guile, reminding Sigurd that he was Sigmund's son, and destined for great deeds. One day when they were speaking in this vein, Regin, with cunning in his heart, told his pupil of a deed that only a hero could perform.

"There is a deed that would right a wrong that was done a long time ago, which at the same time would win you a great treasure that would make you richer than any king of Denmark," he said slyly.

"Tell me more of this matter," demanded Sigurd. "What treasure do you speak of, and what evil is abroad in the land?"

Then Regin spoke slowly and long, telling how he was born of Reidmar, the Ancient, less than the gods but greater than mankind, who gave rare gifts and strange powers to his sons. To Fafnir, the eldest, Reidmar gave a fearless soul, a clever and cunning hand and a heart as hard as stone. To Otter he gave the power to hunt and catch any living thing no matter how wild. To Regin, the youngest, he gave skill in every craft but not the ability to enjoy it, the power to recall the past and look to the future, and a heart which would never know peace. To all three sons he gave each the power to change shape at will and take on the form of other living creatures.

The sons of Reidmar grew to manhood. One day three of the gods, Odin, Loki and Haenir, visited the earth and came to Denmark. They rested by the side of a stream where Otter had assumed the shape of an otter in order to hunt for fish. Loki recognised Otter in his water-shape and killed him.

The gods moved on until they came to the hall of Reidmar who accused them of the death of his son and demanded ransom in the form of a vast treasure belonging to Andvari, the dwarf, who lived in a waterfall by the pool where Loki had killed Otter.

So it was Loki who was sent to gather the treasure, which he did by stealth and trickery, forcing Andvari to drain the pool dry, leaving the treasure gleaming in the sunshine — mounds of golden ornaments and jewels. But there was one ring which Andvari tried to hide, and when Loki demanded it of him he warned Loki that the ring had a curse on it and would bring disaster to whoever owned it. In spite of the warning, Loki insisted and put the ring in his pocket before returning with the treasure to Reidmar. When the gods were handing over the hoard Loki warned Reidmar of the curse that the ring carried. Reidmar laughed, took the ring and dismissed the gods.

Immediately the curse began to work, for there grew in the heart of Fafnir a great covetousness. He longed for his father's acquired treasure, and knew that he would commit murder for it. The more Reidmar gloated over his gold, the more Fafnir lusted after it. Then one night the vision of untold riches blotted all else from Fafnir's eyes. He took his sword and smote his father. Reidmar's death-cry woke Regin who ran from his bed into the hall to find his brother, Fafnir, standing in his father's blood, his sword and his hand bathed red, the heap of treasure spotted with crimson.

A dreadful voice called from the body of Fafnir: "I have spilt the blood of my father. The treasure is mine alone. From this day forward I shall not be parted from my gold and I shall be king of my treasure-heap."

In one night he moved the gold to a rocky cave. Then he changed himself into a dragon of immense length. His coils wallowed through mountains of gold, his breath was a warning fire and smoke from his nostrils filled the cavern of doom.

As he told this tale Regin's voice honeyed with greed and longing. "Now that treasure should be mine. You, Sigurd, son of the Volsungs, can win the treasure and lift the curse. Then the world will become young again, and I shall have honour in the land of my father."

Sigurd listened to this tale with wonder in his heart, and a determination grew in his breast. "You shall have your way. The treasure I will win back, but the curse is yours; take it as you will!"

The next day he went to Regin and said, "You have given me a quest that is worthy of a hero. I have a horse; now you must forge me a sword, also worthy of a hero."

So Regin made Sigurd a sword. Its blade was sharp and cold, like ice that forms over deep water. Its hilt glowed ruby red, and it was worked with runes. Sigurd took the sword, raised it high and smote the anvil on which it had been shaped. The blade shivered, then splintered into fragments like slivers of ice.

Two days and two nights passed before Regin's second sword was ready. It was keener and colder and even more beautifully fashioned than the first. Again Sigurd dashed it against the anvil, and again it turned into shredded ice.

The next day Sigurd went to his mother. "Where are the pieces of my father's sword, the shards he asked you to keep? Where have you hidden them?"

Hiordis led her son to the queen's treasury. There, carefully wrapped in a fine linen cloth lay the shards of the sword given to Sigmund by Odin. Not one spot of rust had been allowed to spoil the lustre of the pieces, and the jewelled hilt flashed strange lights in the chamber.

"Mother, Mother, how faithfully you have kept my father's trust to you. Now your responsibility is mine. I shall have a sword that will shake the throne of kings and release treasure-troves around the world. These pieces will be freshly forged and they will carve a new chapter in the history of the Volsungs!" Sigurd kissed his mother, his face shining with eagerness and anticipation. Hiordis watched him go with love in her heart.

Straight to Regin went Sigurd. The smith took the pieces and toiled over them. He fanned the fire of his forge to a white heat. The shards of Sigmund's sword were like polar-ice and on the anvil they melded together and were reborn. The fire took the newly fashioned blade and water tempered it. At last the sword was ready: it flashed like lightning when Sigurd raised it and smote the anvil with a mighty stroke. It was then that Sigurd cried out. The sharpness of the blade was as keen as it was when it first emerged from the water tank; but the anvil had split in two.

Regin led Sigurd to the river which was flowing full and fast. Casting a lock of fine-spun wool into the current Regin held the sword in its path. When the wool met the blade it was cut cleanly in two. Sigurd called the sword Wrath, saying that his wrath would lead him to great deeds, and even today the sword is known by that name.

So with his horse Greyfell and his sword Wrath, Sigurd set out on the mission to kill Fafnir and retrieve Andvari's treasure. First he visited Gripir to profit from his great wisdom, and the sage gave him his blessing. Then, with Regin to guide him, Sigurd went forth.

Through dark and gloomy forests and over harsh, treacherous mountains they toiled. A mountain pass took them westward past dark and fathomless lakes devoid of life. By day they were scorched by the sun and at night foul and poisonous vapours rose from the earth around them.

After three days Sigurd looked ahead through the grey dawn and spied a desolate land, barren of all growth as far as his eye could see. This he knew was the Glittering Heath where he would find the lair of Fafnir. Leaving Regin behind, Sigurd strode across the desert place strong and confident that the deed would be done that day. As for Regin, only time would tell what good or evil would come to him.

As Sigurd made his way he thought he saw a grey shadow ahead, but when he approached, the figure of a man emerged—one-eyed, bearded and very old, wearing a worn cloak and a hat turned up at one side; but his face shone with the glory of the gods.

The stranger hailed Sigurd by name, "Where do you go with that sword of yours?" he enquired.

"To the lair of the dragon and the house of gold. But hail to you, Ancient One, friend of mine and friend to my father!" replied Sigurd.

"Do you intend to slay the dragon?" asked the Old One.

"With Wrath, my sword, forged from my father's sword," said Sigurd.

"Then take my advice," cautioned the stranger. "No man can approach the dragon face to face, for if you try, the flames from his mouth will devour you. What good would your Wrath be then? No. Go on your way until you come to a deep, hollow track through the desert. That is the path of the dragon. Dig yourself a hole in that track and hide there with your sword drawn until Fafnir passes over. Then you can pierce him through."

"I shall do as you say and I give you thanks and praise, O Mighty One, who appears before me and watches over me," affirmed Sigurd.

"One thing more," added the Ancient. "Remember that the dragon's blood has miraculous properties. Listen not to what Regin tells you. It will not burn or harm you. Rather it will protect you. When you have killed the monster bathe in its blood and wherever it touches you there you will become invulnerable to any weapon on earth or beyond." With those words the stranger vanished.

Sigurd went forward and, as the Ancient One had foretold, he came to the dragon's track. He dug a deep pit and there he waited like one dead and buried, with his sword drawn.

Soon there was a rumbling and a shaking. The air turned black and the smell of brimstone, like hell-fire, hung heavily and filled the pit. Flames like battle torches shot along the track. Slowly the belly of the serpent slid across the opening of the pit. The stench was almost intolerable, the rattle of the dragon's scales was like a hammer on an anvil. All light was blotted out.

In the fetid darkness of the pit, Sigurd thrust upward with all his might. He felt the blade of Wrath pierce the scales as it had sliced the anvil in Regin's forge, and then he knew that he had reached the dark heart of the monster. With a fearsome cry Fafnir yielded up his spirit, and died.

Blood gushed from the wound and cascaded into the pit. Mindful of the advice of the Old One, Sigurd stripped and let the blood shower down upon him. Except where a leaf dislodged by the dragon fell and stuck between his shoulders, Sigurd was washed in the dragon's blood. With his sword the hero dug his way out of the pit and stood by the body of the dragon, Greyfell beside him.

So they stood when Regin came hurrying up. He was both excited and downcast. "There lies the body of my brother whom you have slain," he said.

"Then take his treasure as my ransom," said Sigurd.

"He was still my bother, however evil," said Regin. "So now you shall be my cook and bake my brother's heart that I might eat of it and live to be your master, for Fafnir's heart contains knowledge, power and wisdom." Then Regin sank to the ground exhausted and fell into a seeming sleep.

Sigurd cut out the heart of Fafnir with Wrath and built a fire on which to roast it. Above him eagles wheeled and cried, but he paid no heed. After a while he reached forward with his hand to see that the heart was indeed cooking. When he did so the fat of the heart spat at him, and blood darkened his finger. As men do, he sucked at his finger to cool it. So the blood of the dragon was in his mouth and covered his palate. Even as the blood touched his tongue a miracle occurred. It was as though an inner ear opened inside Sigurd's head and he was able to understand the cry of the birds and, like the dwarfs of old, he could hear what the beasts were saying. In that instant he grew wise in their ways.

Above him the eagles still wheeled but now he heard what they were crying: "Regin has brought a prince of the Volsungs to this place, and now he will kill him so that he himself might live without shame or fear, and with Fafnir's treasure."

Quickly Sigurd turned. Regin had woken from his sleep and his sword was raised to strike Sigurd down. But Sigurd was too quick. Wrath flashed through the air and Regin's head was cleft from his body. So there in the desert the body of Regin lay alongside that of his brother, Fafnir the dragon.

Sigurd himself ate the dragon's heart and grew wise in the wisdom of the dwarfs of ancient times. Then he mounted Greyfell and followed the dragon's tracks to its lair where the treasure of Andvari gleamed even in the darkest recesses of the cave. Atop the glittering pile shone the cursed ring of Andvari, which Loki had wanted for his own. With laughter on his lips the son of Sigmund slipped the ring on his finger and began to pile up treasure ready to load on to his horse, Greyfell. But once again the voice of the eagles came to him, "Leave the gold where it is—there is treasure of another sort at Hindfell. Go and claim it."

Sigurd thought a while, then with Wrath by his side he sprang into the saddle. Greyfell tossed his head and sped across the Glittering Heath, over the desert to where the mountains rose abruptly out of the earth. Swiftly horse and rider scaled the precipice and left far behind them the place of dread where Fafnir had guarded his treasure for so many years.

How Sigurd awoke Brynhild upon Hindfell

Seated upon Greyfell, Sigurd travelled far from the Glittering Heath and Fafnir's treasure-lair. Early one morning his eyes turned to a craggy mountain top which loomed out of the dawn mists. In that light it seemed to Sigurd that a torch burned brightly through the wreath of clouds, a torch that beckoned Sigurd forward. With a neigh Greyfell stretched out his head and began the ascent of the mountain to where the strange light flickered and called.

By noon the clouds gathered in close and thickened, hiding the light that shone atop the mountain. Nevertheless, even though he couldn't see it Sigurd felt the pull of the flare. In the late afternoon a wind sprang up and the clouds dispersed so that Sigurd could once more see the top of the mountain. But now the light was not so much a flare as a ribbon of fire wound around the head of the mountain, Hindfell, which shone like an island in a blazing sea. Rising from the island was a castle, the like of which Sigurd had never before seen.

Greyfell felt his rider's excitement and eagerly topped crest after crest, ascending the mountain with nimble leaps and strides. Closer and closer they came to the fire in the sky which now appeared to be a wall of flame. Even as they breasted the wall neither horse nor rider faltered.

With a daring leap Greyfell burst through the fiery curtain whose flames licked at Sigurd's clothing and ran along Greyfell's mane. Yet neither of the two were in any way burned or harmed. Suddenly the flames subsided like a flare that had been doused and all was quiet and still. The mountainside of Hindfell was no longer ablaze but the earth around Sigurd was scorched. A pale ash covered the surface, laying in wreaths through which Greyfell picked his way.

Before them loomed a wall emblazoned with a hundred shields, every one shining and flawless, gleaming down on the horse and rider. At the wall's pinnacle a shield more ornate and more brilliant than the rest hung like a pennant, swinging slightly in the breeze.

Sigurd sprang lightly from his mount and, approaching the castle wall, he made his way around the ramparts until he came to the great gate. Its doors, wide open, seemed to invite him inside. Upon entering the courtyard Sigurd looked about him. Before him was a marble platform surrounded by slender arched pillars of exquisite proportions, giving the appearance of drapery surrounding the platform. In the centre of the platform was a raised bier, wonderfully ornamented, on which lay the image of a warrior, clad from head to toe in a coat of glittering mail. As Sigurd approached he saw that the head itself was masked by a beautiful wrought helmet, and on the ground beside the image rested a spear and a shield. To Sigurd it seemed that a kingly warrior lay in state, though strangely alone and unguarded.

Stepping forward and sinking to one knee he examined the helmet more closely. Through the eye slits he saw what looked like eyebrows, but when he peered more closely he saw that it was fine silver wire made to look like eyebrows. Then he gently moved the visor and saw that the face beneath was smooth and hairless. The cheeks were fair and rounded, the lips slightly parted, and a gentle breath rose and fell indicating a deep and peaceful sleep.

This was the breath of a woman, beautiful beyond all imagining! Even more carefully Sigurd removed the helmet and the corn-coloured hair beneath fell free. Still the maiden breathed, obviously under a spell and in a trance. The hero touched her and spoke softly, but she didn't respond. Love entered Sigurd's heart and he felt a great tenderness surge through his body. Carefully he took his sword and lightly pierced the coat of mail at the neck to free the head of the sleeping girl; then he ran the point of his sword down the length of the coating of mail so that it fell away to reveal a shift of pure white linen.

With a great feeling of tenderness, Sigurd brushed her lips with his . . . and, much to his astonishment, the maiden awoke! Her eyes travelled across his face and took in every detail of his handsome form. Then she sat up and faced him.

"Who are you? From whence do you come to waken me from sleep?" she asked.

"I am from the world over which Odin dwells. I am of the earth and have crossed the Glittering Heath and scaled many mountains to find you."

While he spoke the sun blazed from the sky and the shields that hung on the castle wall caught its rays and almost blinded the man and the maid. The woman lifted her hands to the sun as though to embrace it. In a clear voice she hailed the day, the sun and the light that had come to her after a long night of sleeping.

Then the two embraced. Love and joy filled their hearts. Sigurd held her to him and she breathed his name; an intonation to life.

"Who are you?" Sigurd asked of her. "What is your name and what is the meaning of your long sleep upon the mountain top?"

Then the maid told him that she was called Brynhild; that she was born of earth folk but that Odin had called her and made her one of his Valkyries, and that she had displeased him during one of his battles by disobeying his wishes and allowing the wrong man to win. So Odin had condemned her to return to earth where she must marry the first mortal she met, no matter how gross or disagreeable he might be. When Brynhild begged for mercy Odin relented, but said, "Let it be. First slumber long beneath the Thorn of Sleep, and when you wake you will love — whoever he might be."

Then, on the crest of Hindfell, Brynhild took Sigurd's hand. The two looked and loved, and together climbed Hindfell to its very top. Far beneath them spread the kingdoms of men. Among them was the land of Lymdale that lay between the woodlands and the sea. There Brynhild had been born.

"Behold the land of my birth," she said. "I shall await you here. Go, do what you have to do, then come to me."

"That, I will do," affirmed Sigurd, and as he spoke he took off Andvari's ring and slipped it on the finger of his beloved. Gladness filled their hearts, and it was morning when Sigurd wended his way down the mountainside to the world waiting below.

When Sigurd placed Andvari's ring on the finger of Brynhild he thought not of the curse which the ring bore. That curse quickly began to take effect, and it was long years before the lovers were to meet again, and then only as strangers. For after Sigmund left Brynhild behind on Hindfell his journey took him to the land of an evil witch-queen, Grimhild, who sweetened his wine with a potion and wove a spell. As the queen fixed Sigurd with her eye and spoke softly to him his brain clouded, he forgot that Brynhild existed and he saw Grimhild's lovely daughter Gudrun. Held by the witch's spell, Sigurd married Gudrun, who loved him dearly.

But Grimhild's evil heart was not content. Weaving another spell, she sent Sigurd and her son, Gunnar, back through the flames of Hindfell to where Brynhild, wearing the cursed ring, slept once more. Gunnar immediately fell in love with her and persuaded Sigurd, who was still under the enchantment of Grimhild's spell, to change shapes with him. So Sigurd appeared in the likeness of Gunnar, and Gunnar took on the appearance of Sigurd.

Then Sigurd, in the likeness of Gunnar, approached the sleeping Brynhild, woke her and claimed the ring. So the first shape that Brynhild saw upon waking was that of Gunnar. Thus she was tricked into marrying Gunnar, and went to live at the court of Queen Grimhild. There, life was full of discord caused by the Queen's scheming and the curse of the ring which Gunnar had taken.

When Gunnar's other brothers, driven by the hatred that filled the palace, murdered Sigurd by stabbing him in the back between the shoulder blades — the one place where the dragon's blood had not reached — his body was burnt on a huge funeral pyre. It was then that Brynhild recognised Sigurd as her true lover and husband. Rather than live without him she plunged Sigurd's sword into her heart. Thus she joined him in the fire, with the sword between them. Together they went to Odin in Valhalla; and the ring of Andvari passed into the hands of greedy men.

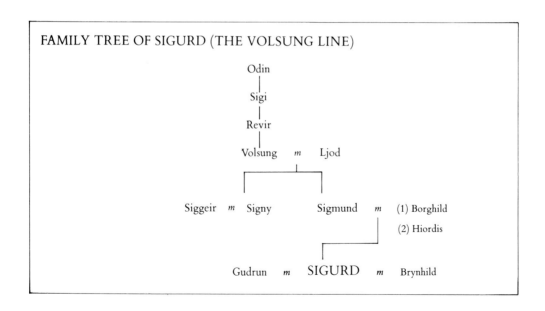

FAMILY TREE OF SIGURD (THE VOLSUNG LINE)

Odin

Sigi

Revir

Volsung *m* Ljod

Siggeir *m* Signy   Sigmund *m* (1) Borghild
                                             (2) Hiordis

Gudrun *m* SIGURD *m* Brynhild

Vainamoinen: Hero, Singer and Enchanter

Early in the nineteenth century a Finnish doctor called Elias Lönnrot developed a deep interest in the old hero tales and songs — or *runot* — sung by his people. He travelled the countryside collecting these fragments and gradually developed the theory that they could be pieced together to reform an ancient Finnish epic poem. He worked on his project for many years, and in 1849 he ordered his collected *runot* into a long epic poem, the form and metre of which Henry Longfellow later used when writing his epic poem, *Hiawatha*.

Kalevala, meaning Land of the Heroes, was the home of the three Finnish heroes: Vainamoinen — singer of songs, who sang the world into being; Ilmarinen — skilful smith; and Lemminkainen — the harebrained rogue. Their adventures are told in song rather than prose, and unlike so many heroes they are not warriors, renowned for mighty deeds in battle. Rather they are magicians, given to song, who journey far and make miraculous escapes by magic. Although they are god-like they have the human frailties of pride and deceit, so must ultimately depart the earthly world. At the end of the epic, Vainamoinen's leaving of Kalevala is not only tragically and hauntingly beautiful but it is an almost elegaic lament to the passing of the old gods as the influence of Christianity comes to Finland.

Vainamoinen, who was old from the day he was born having been thirty years in the womb, was the son of Ilmatar, the creator earth-mother. He was the greatest of all singers, and through his songs he could cast spells and destroy his enemies. It was he who invented the zither, an ancient musical instrument. He fashioned it from the bones of fish and animals together with animal hair and hide. At his playing the world of nature was flooded with joy and gladness. Storm and tempest were stilled and the elements came under his control; wild animals became tame. His music brought harmony to a troubled world.

91

Like so many heroes his life was a series of labours. One of the first occurred when Joukahainen challenged him to a singing contest. Because of the magical charm of his song Vainamoinen was easily the victor, and as the prize Joukahainen offered his sister, Aino, to be the singer's bride. But Aino shivered at the thought of marrying such an old man and rather than submit to such a fate she plunged herself into a stormy lake and descended to the gloomy realm of Ahto, the water lord. Vainamoinen, mourning her loss, rowed out on to the lake in search of his bride, where she appeared to him in the form of a salmon and told him that she could never leave the kingdom of Ahto.

Disconsolate, Vainamoinen, mounted on a stallion whose enchanted shoes bore him swiftly over land and sea, journeyed to the desolate land of Pohja in search of a bride. But his enemy, Joukahainen, waited for him and shot him with a great bow. The hero tumbled into the sea where he drifted for nine days until he was rescued by an eagle who carried him to the cold wastes of Pohja. Vainamoinen arrived chilled to the core of his being, his long beard iced to his breast and his feet frozen in his boots. He was greeted by Old Louhi, a terrifying enchantress, the mistress of Pohja, who struck a bargain. If he could fashion a *sampo*, a mill, to her impossible requirement, then she would not only see that he returned home to his cornfields safely but she would give him her daughter to be his wife.

Vainamoinen knew that there was only one person who could forge such a mill as Old Louhi demanded. That was Ilmarinen, the smith who had forged heaven itself. So Vainamoinen struck a bargain, and Old Louhi sent him on his way with the promise that he would bring Ilmarinen to her. But there was one thing Vainamoinen must not do. On the journey he must look neither to the right nor the left, neither above nor below — but always straight ahead.

At the foot of the rainbow Vainamoinen forgot his promise and raised his eyes to follow its arch. There he saw the maiden of Pohja, Old Louhi's daughter, and he tried to entice her into his sledge. When she set him the task of splitting a hair with a blunt knife that had no point, he sang to the knife and charmed it to do his bidding. When she bade him tie a knot in an egg so that the knot could not be seen, he charmed a serpent into the egg which tied itself into knots. Everything she commanded he did, but still the maiden would not join him in the sledge. Then she promised to come if only he would carve a boat from the splinter of her spindle and launch it without touching it.

Vainamoinen took his axe and worked at the splinter of the maiden's spindle, all the while singing a boat into being. But while he was still working, Hiisi, the Evil One, turned aside the axe so that Vainamoinen was sorely wounded. The ship faded away as the blood of the hero flowed to the ground; and as the ship passed from sight, so too did the maiden.

Vainamoinen was near dying of his wounds when he met an old man who sang

magical songs of water, fire and iron. When the man sang of iron, the wound from the iron axe began to close. The old man sang songs of healing until the wound was completely healed, and Vainamoinen could pursue his way.

His way led him to Ilmarinen, his friend, the smith who had forged the heavens, and whom he had promised to send to Old Louhi.

It took great persuasion and magic on the part of Vainamoinen, but at last Ilmarinen went to Old Louhi and promised to forge her the *sampo* that would grind out prosperity. Ilmarinen built his furnace and set up his anvil and for seven days he forged the magic ingredients — tips from the feathers of white swans, milk from a barren heifer, a single grain of barley and wool from the fleece of an ewe — while Old Louhi's goblins fanned the fire.

On the evening of the seventh day the mill had been fashioned — a mill that would grind corn or salt or gold. Old Louhi was wildly gleeful. The magic *sampo* was hers. But she did nothing about her payment to Ilmarinen. When he grew impatient the maiden and her mother fobbed him off until he realised that he had been tricked, and went home.

Next, Lemminkainen, the handsome but harebrained rogue, came to woo the maiden, Old Louhi's daughter. Old Louhi set him three tasks: to hunt and catch the elk of Hiisi, the Evil One; to catch Hiisi's chestnut horse; and to shoot the swan of Tuonela.

But even when he completed these tasks the maiden of Pohja was unmoved, and in her heart she determined to marry Ilmarinen.

Meanwhile, Vainamoinen could not forget the maiden and determined to build a boat to carry him back to the icy land of Pohja . . .

Vainamoinen builds a boat and finds the lost words

Vainamoinen's first task was to find a tree that would provide him with suitable timber for the building of his boat. To help him he called upon another hero, Sampsa, the earth-born, and together they journeyed into the forest, but for a long time they failed to find a tree that would do. At last they came upon a mighty oak tree which would serve their purpose well. Bowing low, Sampsa addressed the oak tree courteously and gained permission to fell the tree.

"It is only fit," said the oak, "for I am the finest tree in the forest and my timber will provide a worthy keel for Vainamoinen's boat." So Sampsa dropped the tree and Vainamoinen set to with his axe to fashion a boat that would bear him across the sea to the land of Pohja.

As he worked, Vainamoinen sang, and he fashioned the boat as one makes a song, with harmony and melody so that his hands shaped a fine craft. At last it was finished; but when he looked at it, Vainamoinen knew that he was missing three words that would make all the difference between a fine boat and the finest boat ever seen in that country. Without these three words it would flounder and sink in the first storm.

So he went searching for the words. He looked first among the animals of the woods and in the nests of the birds, but he couldn't find them there.

Perhaps if he could cross the river of death and enter the Kingdom of the Dead he would find them, because every word that has been spoken on earth must some time pass over into that kingdom with the speaker. But to gain entry into the kingdom of the departed he would have to persuade the daughter of Tuoni, king of the Otherworld, to take him there. It was Tuoni's daughter who ferried the dead across the river to their ultimate dwelling place in Tuonela. He would have to pretend to be dead even though he looked very much alive.

The journey to the gloomy river of the dead took him three weeks, and then he had to find the place where Tuoni's daughter took on board her passengers. At last he reached the crossing place and called to the rower in a faltering voice, asking to be taken across the river.

Tuoni's daughter was not easily tricked, and she recognised Vainamoinen's stories for the lies that they were. First he tried to make out that he had died of a disease and had been summoned by Tuoni himself; then that he had been killed by an iron weapon. Each time Tuoni's daughter accused him of deceiving her. So Vainamoinen told her that he had met his death by drowning and she replied that he was a liar. Then he told her that he had been consumed by fire, but she laughed at that story, pointing to his unscorched hair and beard.

So Vainamoinen told the girl the truth, and his honeyed words persuaded her. Grumbling the while, she ferried Vainamoinen across the river to Tuonela. But she warned him that no good would come of the expedition.

And so it seemed to the hero, for he was the first of the living to set foot in that dread place. The handmarks of death were everywhere in that fearful land of shadows. Tuonetar, the queen of Tuonela, met him and gave him sour wine writhing with worms in a foul goblet and asked him why he had come.

When Vainamoinen told her, she shook her head and said that Tuoni would never give him the words. Moreover now that he had made his way to Tuonela he would have to stay there forever. No one ever returns from the Otherworld of the Dead. Vainamoinen, she said, had sung his last earthly song.

The hero pretended to sleep and he searched in his mind for the three words he needed to complete his boat. Although many words whispered themselves in his ear he knew they were not the words he needed. He listened to all the words spoken on earth: far-off unhappy words, joyful words of praise, sweet words of love and the loud harsh words of anger. They were not the words he needed.

While Vainamoinen pretended to sleep, Tuoni commanded a witch-wife to spin threads of iron and a wizard to weave them into a net; this net was stretched across the river so that Vainamoinen could not escape from the kingdom. But Vainamoinen saw what was happening and had no intention in staying in this kingdom forever; so he changed himself into an otter and sank into the river, then he changed into a tiny fish and slipped through the net. He had escaped . . . but still he needed those three words.

He asked the wind, who went everywhere, to help him. The wind asked far and wide, across land and sea, through mountain passes and valleys, brushing the desert sand and sweeping across the plains.

A shepherd heard the wind's questions and passed a message back to Vainamoinen that Antero Vipunen, the monster magician who lived in a far place, stored all the words of the earth in his stomach. The road to Antero Vipunen was the hardest road a man or god could follow, the shepherd warned: it wound its way over a forest of needles sharper than any woman's tongue, then across a plain of razor-like sword blades, and another that was made of hatchets ground to the finest edge. Not an easy road to tread.

Vainamoinen knew that what the shepherd said was true so he went to Ilmarinen, his friend the smith, and asked him to forge a stout pair of iron shoes, a pair of copper gauntlets and a shirt of iron. He would also need a staff of the strongest metal, he explained. Ilmarinen didn't like the sound of his friend's chances, but he did as he was asked and in nine days Vainamoinen was ready for his journey to the dwelling place of Antero Vipunen.

On the first day he easily crossed the forest of needles. His iron shoes saw him safely across the sword blades the second day, and on the third day he ran across the gleaming hatchet edges. Still ahead of him was Antero Vipunen, one of the most ancient and cunning of magicians, with all the words and songs of men stored in his stomach. Out of the shoulder of this old one grew an aspen tree, from each temple grew a birch tree and from his chin an elder. Willows sprouted from his beard, a dark green fir tree from his mouth, and a vast oak tree was rooted in his forehead.

Having made it this far, Vainamoinen approached this awesome sight. He drew his sword and took his axe out of its magic leather scabbard. First he cut down the aspen tree, and one by one he felled the forest that sprouted from the giant's head. With the stout staff that Ilmarinen had forged for him he prised open the mighty jaws of old Antero Vipunen and spoke magic words into the open mouth

of the monster.

"Wake from your long slumber, master of magicians. I have come to ask you something."

Already the torture of Vainamoinen's axe and the iron in his jaw had roused the old one, who bit down hard on Vainamoinen's staff and severed it in two, then opened his mouth in an almighty roar.

Vainamoinen was taken by surprise. He carelessly stepped forward to shout back at the giant and tumbled headlong into that great open mouth, still wearing his shoes and shirt of iron. At that moment the monster swallowed, and Vainamoinen slid easily down the enormous throat.

"I've eaten many things in my day. I've dined on goat, sheep and reindeer, bear, ox, wolf and wild boar, but that is the sweetest meal I've ever had," spoke Antero Vipunen; and he settled down to sleep again.

Vainamoinen, down inside the monster, formed a plan. In his belt he carried a knife with a handle of birch wood. This handle he sang by magic into a boat large enough to hold him. In this vessel he rowed through the entrails of the monster and when he reached the belly he set up a forge. From his iron shirt he made a smithy and used the sleeves for bellows. His knees served as an anvil and for three days the bellows roared and the anvil rang like clashing peals of thunder.

All the tumult inside him roused Antero Vipunen from his dozing and angrily he cried, "What hero have I swallowed? Countless men I've eaten, but never one like you. Smoke comes from my nostrils, my mouth breathes sparks and fire, and my throat is choked with burning cinders. Leave me, evil genius. Go back to where you belong, to the caverns of the white bear, the pit of serpents, the foul swamps of the fenland, the hot-springs of the mountains, or wherever your home is. If you will but leave me I'll give you the swiftest horse of Hiisi, the Evil One, if you demand it. If you don't leave me I'll send eagles to claw you and vultures to tear you apart. So depart and let me sleep."

Vainamoinen listened to this long speech then paused from his hammering and replied, "I'm comfortable enough here. I have plenty to eat and drink. Vainamoinen is content in your belly. Here I shall stay, and I promise you I shall set my forge and bellows deeper and deeper into your innards and I shall swing my hammer against your vital parts—your heart, lungs and liver—until you speak all the words and songs stored around me. Every word you have ever heard I want released until we reach the three magic words I need."

Then this powerful old magician opened his store of knowledge. All the incantations of the ages, songs sung from the first creation, all the sources of good and evil, the orders of enchantment, every tongue that had moved in any language on earth: all these came pouring forth. Never had such singing been heard in the history of the universe. A countless number of songs Vipunen sang.

For three days and three nights he sang. The moon and the stars stopped to listen. Waterfalls were stilled, rivers ceased flowing, the tides rested and the sea-waves waited while Antero Vipunen sang, and words filled the air like all the stars of all the galaxies of the heavens.

When the hero, Vainamoinen, had learned all the magic sayings, the ancient songs and legends and the words of ancient wisdom, the long-lost words of the master, he prepared to leave the body of the magician singer, Vipunen. He spoke, then, to the enchanter: "Now Antero Vipunen, open wide your mouth. I have found the three lost magic words I need, and I will now leave you forever and return to Kalevala."

Then Vipunen answered him. "Many things I've eaten — beast, man and hero; but never anything like you, Vainamoinen. You have got what you came for. You have found the three words of the master. Go now, in peace, and don't ever come back. Take my blessing and go."

As he finished Vipunen opened his mouth wide, then wider, and Vainamoinen straightway left the belly of the enchanter and walked through the open mouth. He journeyed over the hills and vales of the Northland to the plains of Kalevala and to the smithy of his brother-hero, Ilmarinen. There the smith, the artist-in-iron, asked Vainamoinen if he had found the long-lost wisdom, the secret doctrine and the words of magic.

And Vainamoinen replied that he had. "I have learned all the words of the world's store, the incantations of the ages, the words of ancient wisdom and I have found the long-lost words of the master."

So Vainamoinen the magic-builder went to where his boat was hidden in the place where he had worked so cunningly. Now he had the three magic words. The boat could be completed, built only by magic. The tasks set by the maiden of Pohja who sat on the arch of the rainbow had been completed.

Afterwards Vainamoinen sailed to Pohja but the maiden still refused to marry him. Instead she chose Ilmarinen; and a great wedding feast was held, but it was not long before the maiden died. Later Ilmarinen married the maiden's sister, but it was an unhappy marriage. Ilmarinen turned his wife into a seagull and sought revenge on Old Louhi, the mother who had sided against him.

Ilmarinen determined to steal the magic *sampo* of prosperity and he asked Lemminkainen and Vainamoinen to help him. On the way to Pohja the heroes killed a huge pike and Vainamoinen fashioned a harp from its jawbone. With the harp he was able to lull Old Louhi to sleep, and the heroes made off with the *sampo*. Old Louhi woke up and chased them and in the fight over the *sampo* it was broken.

Vainamoinen took the broken pieces of the *sampo* and planted them in Kalevala. There they brought prosperity to the land. But Old Louhi would not rest, and she worked against Vainamoinen. She sent a bear to attack his herds but he killed it, and such were the songs he sang that the sun and the moon stopped to listen to them.

Old Louhi then caught the moon in a net and sang the sun into her head before shutting it up in a dark cavern. Next she put out all the fires in Kalevala so that nothing could grow and the earth would die, a land of perpetual darkness and winter.

Ilmarinen set to work to forge a new moon and a new sun, but they were only toys and they wouldn't shine. So he began to forge chains with which to bind Old Louhi and the heroes threatened to go to Pohja and tether the old witch with an iron collar. Louhi knew then that she was beaten. Bitterly, she released the moon and put back the true sun. The grain began to grow again and the feud between the heroes and Old Louhi was at an end. She stayed in Pohja, and Kalevala prospered once more.

After many episodes and much time, there was born and grew up in the land a girl called Marjatta. Marjatta miraculously conceived a child, and he was delivered in a stable. The child was marked with a cross, the sign that he would be the new king. Vainamoinen knew then that his reign was over, and he sang himself a magical boat of copper which bore him into the sky. As he was taken away, he promised to come again when he was needed.

The Old Testament

The Old Testament of the Bible is a collection of books originally written in Hebrew although parts were written in Aramaic, the official language of the Persian Empire and the ordinary language of Palestine by the time of Christ.

Texts in Old Testament times were written on clay tablets and papyrus or leather scrolls. These "scrolls" became the "books" of the Old Testament. They were written from right to left and often stored in stone jars for safe keeping. In 1946–47 a shepherd working on the hillsides close to the Dead Sea found a cave in which were hidden a number of jars containing what are now known as the Dead Sea Scrolls. These proved to be the earliest copies of the Old Testament ever discovered.

Like those of the Greeks, Babylonians and Vikings, the Old Testament stories were passed on by word of mouth before being written down. The Old Testament itself is a library of books recording the history of the Children of Israel, or the Jewish people as we know them today.

The first five books, called the Pentateuch, trace the history of the Jews from Abraham — the father of the Jewish nation — to Joseph — the Jewish boy who would rise to rule at the right hand of the Pharoah in Egypt — with an introduction explaining the origin of the world and the beginning of evil in the human race. The Pentateuch tells of the growth of civilisation and, because it contains the fundamental rules of moral conduct — the Ten Commandments — along with detailed instructions for everyday living, the Jews call it "The Book of the Law" or "Sefer Torah".

The next twelve books are historical and develop the story of the Jews until they were defeated by the Babylonians and Persians and sent into exile, and, later, their return from exile. There are also five books of drama, poetry and song and seventeen books of prophecy.

Dominating the entire structure of the Old Testament is the presence of the unseen one true God whose name was not to be spoken, but who was referred to in the sacred writings as YHWH, or Yahweh—the Lord.

Like every other people the Jews told wonderful stories of their heroes and prophets. The drama of their stories arises from the hero's obedience or disobedience to Yahweh. Because of the strict rules of Jewish behaviour and the worship of Yahweh, even the greatest of the heroes became fallible. The stories of their exploits include their weaknesses as well as their triumphs.

Under the protection of Joseph the statesman and the Pharoah who favoured him, the patriarch Jacob—father of Joseph—and his family settled in Egypt. It was Moses who later led the children of Israel out of Egypt to resettle in Canaan, which they took by force. In Canaan they were oppressed by the Philistines against whom they eventually revolted. Led by David, the Jews defeated the Philistines and established a royal house, David becoming the first king of Israel.

Moses the Lawgiver

Under the rule of Joseph of Egypt, a great company of Jacob's descendants, who were called Israelites or Hebrews, were allowed to settle in the country; and there they lived and prospered. After Joseph and the Pharoah whom he served died there was left in Egypt a large community of Israelites.

Then there came to the throne a pharoah who hadn't known Joseph, and who hated the Israelites because he was afraid that they would fight against him in the event of war. He put the Israelites to work as slaves, making bricks and building great stone cities, wearing them down under heavy loads. Then the king issued a decree that every boy born to the Israelites should be thrown into the River Nile. He thought that in this way there would be no Israelite boys left to grow into fighting men.

At this time there lived in Egypt a Hebrew man and his wife who had two children—a daughter called Miriam and a three-year-old son called Aaron. When another son was born the couple hid him in the house instead of throwing him into the Nile. All was well for three months. Then the child began to cry so loudly that his mother feared that people passing would hear him and report his presence in the house. So she thought up a plan to save his life.

From the river-side she gathered papyrus reeds which she wove into a basket, coating it with pitch and bitumen to make it water-proof. Into the basket she placed her child. She carried the basket to the river and set it into the water among the rushes, leaving Miriam to keep watch from a distance to see what would happen.

Now Pharoah's daughter went to the river to bathe at the very spot where the basket was hidden. When she saw it she sent her maid to fetch it. She opened the basket and was most astonished at what she saw. The baby in the basket began crying and the princess, recognising the marks on the cloth the baby was wrapped in, said to her maid, "This is a Hebrew boy."

As she spoke, Miriam stepped forward and said politely, "Shall I go and call you a nurse from among the Hebrew women to take care of the child for you?"

The princess felt sorry for the babe and, as its rescuer, already felt an attachment to it. "Yes, go," the Pharoah's daughter said to Miriam, and the girl went off to fetch her mother.

When the baby's mother was brought, the princess said to her, "Take this child away and nurse it for me, and I will see that you are paid." And so she did. When the child grew up she took him to Pharoah's daughter, who treated him like a son and called him Moses, because, she said, "I drew him out of the water."

Moses grew up at the court of Pharoah and was treated as a prince, being taught all the wisdom of the Egyptians. Riches and honours were given him and, had he chosen, he could have lived his days in the palace of Pharoah.

But even as a young man he recognised the hard life his countrymen, the Hebrews, were having, for he knew of his true heritage, having been secretly taught by his "nurse". Once, when he saw an Egyptian strike a Hebrew, he looked around and when he saw no one in sight he killed the Egyptian and buried him in the sand.

The next day Moses was again among the workers when he saw two Hebrews fighting. Stepping between them he said to the one who was in the wrong, "What do you mean by hitting your countryman?"

"Who gave you the right to rule over us?" retorted the Hebrew. "Do you intend to kill me as you killed the Egyptian yesterday?"

Moses was frightened because he knew that the matter had come to light and that Pharoah would be after his life, so he fled from Egypt and went to live in the land of Midian . . .

Let my people go

For forty years Moses lived in Midian, where he married and had two sons. He became the keeper of his father-in-law's flocks, and was happy. During this period the king of Egypt died but the new pharoah continued to oppress the Hebrews even more severely, so that they called out to Yahweh, in despair, to deliver them from their slavery.

Now one day Moses led his flock to the other side of the wilderness to a place called Horeb, the Mountain of God. There, an angel of Yahweh appeared to him in the shape of a flame of fire which sprang from the heart of a bush. Even as Moses looked the bush blazed with light but was not burnt up. When he stepped forward to look more closely a voice called his name, "Moses! Moses!"

"Here I am," answered Moses.

"Don't come any closer," said the voice, "but take off your shoes, for the ground you stand on is holy ground."

Moses recognised the voice of God and hid his face in his hands. And the voice continued: "I have seen the miserable state of the Israelites and heard their cry. So I have decided to send you to Pharoah to bring the Hebrew people, the Israelites, out of Egypt."

"Who am I to go to Pharoah with such a demand?" asked Moses.

"I shall be with you," came the answer, "and after you have freed my people, you are to offer worship to God on this mountain."

"But what if no one believes me?" asked Moses.

"What is that in your hand?" asked the voice.

"A staff," said Moses.

"Throw it on the ground," commanded the voice.

So Moses threw his staff on to the ground, and it turned into a serpent.

"Now pick it up!"

And Moses picked up the serpent and it turned back into a staff.

"Put your hand into your bosom," came the voice again. Moses put his hand into his bosom and when he drew it out it was covered with leprosy like snow.

"Put your hand back into your bosom."

This time when Moses drew it out it was clean and new, just like the rest of his flesh.

Even after these omens Moses was not convinced and he said to Yahweh, "My lord, I have never been an eloquent man. Rather, I am slow of speech. How will I be able to speak convincingly?"

"Then your brother Aaron can speak for you. He is an eloquent man and will come to meet you. He will be your mouthpiece and you will speak through him like a god. Now, take this staff in your hand, for with it you will perform miracles." Then the light disappeared from the bush and the voice was heard no more at Horeb.

As Moses set out across the wilderness to Egypt he was met by his brother Aaron who led him to the Hebrew people, and when Moses showed them the signs, they were convinced that he had come to deliver them from the scourge of Pharoah.

So Moses and Aaron went to Pharoah and said, "Yahweh, the God of the Israelites, bids us come to you with the command: 'Let my people go, so that they can keep a feast in the wilderness in honour of me.'"

Pharoah was not willing to understand the message. He saw the many thousands of slaves who were building his cities and his tombs and he would not believe that there was anyone strong enough to deliver them out of his powerful hand. So he asked scornfully, "Who is this lord, that I should obey his voice?"

At that Aaron threw down his staff and it became a serpent.

So Pharoah summoned his sages and sorcerers who with their wizardry did the same. Each threw down his staff and it turned into a serpent. Then Aaron's staff swallowed up the staffs of the magicians. But even so Pharoah would not listen to Moses and Aaron.

Aaron then took his staff in his hand and stretched it over all the waters of Egypt: the rivers and their canals, the marshlands and the reservoirs, every tub and jar; and the water everywhere turned into blood, so that it was impossible for the Egyptians to drink water for seven days.

Still Pharoah refused to let the people go.

So Aaron stretched out his staff again and the country was plagued with frogs. The river swarmed with them; they made their way into the palace; they even got into ovens and kneading bowls. They climbed all over the people, even the courtiers in the palace. This time Pharoah promised that if the frogs were removed he would let the Israelites go, but when Moses used his power to pile up the frogs in heaps Pharoah changed his mind and refused to keep his promise.

This time Aaron, at Moses's command, stretched out his staff and a swarm of mosquitoes attacked both man and beast throughout Egypt. The magicians also tried to produce mosquitoes but they failed. Still Pharoah refused to listen to Moses.

So followed plague after plague. After the mosquitoes came the gadflies. Then all the Egyptians' livestock were struck with a deadly plague; when Aaron took a handful of soot from a kiln and threw it in the air, boils broke out on men and beasts. The land was struck with hail and what survived the hail was eaten by locusts. Still Pharoah would not let the sons and daughters of Israel go.

Then Moses stretched his hand toward heaven and a darkness so thick that it could be felt covered Egypt. Even then Pharoah was stubborn and refused to let the Israelites leave Egypt.

Only after all this did Moses instruct his people, the community of Israel, in exact terms. On the tenth day of the month each man was to take a male animal one year old and without blemish from his flock, one for each family. On the fourteenth day of the month the animals were to be slaughtered and some of the blood was to be taken and smeared on the two doorposts and the lintel of the houses. The animal was to be eaten roasted over the fire of the house and served with herbs and unleavened bread.

The people were to eat the meal hastily, for this was to be a passover meal eaten between sunset and darkness. That night Yahweh would go through the land of Egypt and the first-born male of every family, man and beast, would die;

but when Yahweh saw the blood on the doorposts and lintels he would pass over that homestead. This would be a day to be remembered by the children of Israel forever.

At midnight, after the sacrifice of the Passover, just as Moses had predicted Yahweh struck down all the first-born males in the land of Egypt, from the first-born of Pharoah himself to the first-born of the prisoners in his dungeon.

It was still night when Pharoah summoned Moses and Aaron and said, 'Take the sons and daughters of Israel and get out of the land. Go and offer worship to Yahweh as you have asked. Take your flocks and your herds, but go and go quickly before we are all dead.''

Moses lost no time gathering his people together in a vast army and they left Egypt, fully armed, by a route which led to the Sea of Reeds; and an angel went before them in the form of a pillar of fire by night and a pillar of cloud by day.

Back in Egypt, Pharoah soon regretted his decision and the loss of his slave labour. He gathered an army of horsemen and gave chase, taking his chariots to where the Israelites were camped by the sea.

Then the angel who marched at the front of the Israelites changed to the rear so that a pillar of cloud stood between the Egyptians and the Israelites. Moses stretched out his hand over the sea, causing it to be driven back all night by a strong easterly wind. The waters parted so that the Israelite people could move ahead on dry land, with a wall of water on either side.

The Egyptians, seeing this incredible walkway, gave chase right into the sea—all of Pharoah's horses, his chariots and his horsemen—but the sand clogged the chariot wheels and they made slow progress. Only after the Israelites were safely across on the further shore did Moses again stretch out his hand. This time the waters rolled back, overwhelming the army of Pharoah so that not a single man survived.

Miriam, the prophetess and sister of Moses, took up a timbrel and all the Hebrew women followed her dancing and singing: "Sing of Yahweh: he has covered himself with glory. Horse and rider he has thrown into the sea."

And the people venerated Yahweh and put their faith in Moses, his servant.

The Ten Commandments

Three months after their escape from Egypt the children of Israel reached the wilderness of Sinai. There they pitched camp, facing the mountain which was also called Sinai. From that mountain Moses heard the voice of Yahweh, the God of the Israelites, calling him.

So Moses went up the mountain and brought down to his people a message from Yahweh. If the Israelites promised to obey the voice of Yahweh and keep his laws they would become a nation set aside to serve only Yahweh. And the people promised to do this.

A second time Moses ascended the mountain. There the voice of Yahweh instructed him to tell the people to wash their clothes and prepare themselves for the third day. No one was to go up the mountain or even to touch the foot of it, but when the ram's horn sounded a loud blast they were to go up to the mountain where Yahweh himself would speak.

At daybreak on the third day, thunder pealed and lightning flashed from the mountain which was covered with dense cloud. A trumpet blast was heard, so loud that the people trembled.

Then Moses led the people out of the camp to meet Yahweh at the foot of the mountain. The mountain itself was wrapped entirely in smoke through which shot flashes of fire. Louder and louder came the sound of the trumpet and the mountain shook violently. Moses called out and Yahweh answered him in loud peals of thunder, calling him to ascend to the summit of the mountain.

At the top of Mount Sinai Yahweh spoke to Moses telling him to mark the limits of the mountain so that no one could approach it, for this was sacred ground. Not even the priests, but only Moses and Aaron were to pass beyond the boundaries set out by Moses.

All the people trembled and stood back from the mountain much afraid of the loud peals of thunder, the flashes of lightning, the smoke and the trumpet blast. While they kept their distance Moses approached the thick cloud where Yahweh was.

The cloud grew even thicker and covered the mountain for six days. On the seventh day Yahweh called Moses from inside the cloud. To the people below it seemed that the mountain top was blazing with fire. Moses went right into the cloud and stayed there for forty days and forty nights.

Hidden by the veil of cloud Moses inscribed on two stone tablets the laws which Yahweh dictated to him. For this was to be the law by which the children of Israel would be governed.

YOU SHALL HAVE NO OTHER GODS EXCEPT ME.

YOU SHALL NOT WORSHIP IDOLS.

YOU SHALL NOT MISUSE THE NAME OF YAHWEH.

REMEMBER THE SABBATH DAY AND KEEP IT HOLY.

HONOUR YOUR FATHER AND YOUR MOTHER.

YOU SHALL NOT KILL.

YOU SHALL NOT COMMIT ADULTERY.

YOU SHALL NOT STEAL.

YOU SHALL NOT BEAR FALSE WITNESS AGAINST YOUR NEIGHBOUR.

YOU SHALL NOT COVET.

For forty years Moses led the people through the wilderness to the Promised Land of Canaan where the Israelites would settle. During that time he refined and codified a complex set of laws, which are all recorded in the Old Testament of the Bible.

But Moses was not to enjoy the Promised Land himself. At the journey's end he climbed Mount Nebo, the peak of Pisgah opposite Jericho, the city of palm trees, and Yahweh showed him the land where his people would dwell. But because, during the forty-year journey, Moses had broken faith with Yahweh and had not kept himself utterly holy, he was not permitted to enter Canaan.

So Moses, his eyes undimmed and his great energy unabated, died on Mount Nebo in the land of Moab. There he was buried in a valley, but no one has ever found his grave.

For thirty days the people mourned, for never had there been such a prophet in Israel as Moses.

Samson the Nazirite

After the death of Moses the Israelites, led by Joshua, who had been Moses's commander, crossed the river Jordan, conquered the city of Jericho and settled in the land of Canaan; but not without a struggle.

For many years the Israelites fought constantly with other occupants of the area. Their chief opponents were the Philistines, sometimes called the Sea People because they had crossed the sea from the Greek mainland and Aegean Islands. After many battles the Philistines had settled in five city-states along the southern coast of Canaan. This was about the end of the thirteenth century B.C.

Because they were not satisfied with their narrow strip of land, the Philistines attempted to push inland. This brought them into conflict with the Israelites, who were not united but divided into tribes, each with its own territory. The Philistines had iron weapons and a strong army. For forty years they dominated Israel and two of the tribes, Dan and Judah, fought for their very existence.

During this period when the Israelites were oppressed by the warlike Philistines, there was a man and his wife of the tribe of Dan who had no children. When at last they had a son they called him Samson.

Before the baby was born an angel appeared to his mother and father and said, "You must never allow your son to drink wine or any strong drink, and you must never cut his hair, because God wants him for a Nazirite — a very great honour. Your son, when he becomes a man, will deliver your people from the Philistines."

"What is your name," asked Manoah, the father, "so that we can honour you?"

"My name is a mystery," replied the angel. "You do not need to know."

So Manoah killed a goat and offered it up as a sacrifice to his God. As the flames leapt heavenward the angel ascended in the flame in the sight of Manoah and his wife, who fell face downward on the ground. For they knew that a great honour had come to them, the parents of Samson the Nazirite.

113

The downfall of Samson the rebel

The young Samson grew quickly and even as a boy became very strong — the strongest youth of his tribe. So strong was he that one day he seized a lion by the jaw and tore it to pieces, as if it was only a young lamb or a kid. Not long afterwards he noticed that there was a swarm of bees in the lion's carcass and that they had made honey. He took some of the honey in his hand and ate it as he walked along.

But Samson was hated by the Philistines who oppressed his people, because of his strength and his fierce ways. He once went down into one of their cities and killed thirty of their people. Another time he caught three hundred foxes, took some torches and tied the foxes tail to tail with a torch between each pair. Then he lit the flares and set the foxes loose in the cornfields of the Philistines. In this way he burnt not only the standing corn and the sheaves already harvested, but grape vines and olive trees as well.

When the Philistines saw that their harvest was destroyed, they marched into the Israelites' land and demanded that Samson be given up to them. Samson allowed his fellow Israelites to bind him with two new cords and even permitted himself to be delivered to the camp of the Philistines. Inside the camp, even as the Philistines were running toward him with triumphant shouts, Samson stretched out his arms and the ropes fell away as though they were no stronger than straw or string. Samson then picked up from the ground the jawbone of an ass and began to use it as a sword. Almost a thousand men he struck down with this weapon.

It was after this that Samson fell in love with a Philistine woman called Delilah. When the Philistine rulers heard that Samson was coming often to visit the woman they went secretly to her and said: "Try to wheedle out of Samson the secret of his great strength. If you help us capture him we will reward you handsomely."

So when Samson once again visited Delilah she asked him: "Please tell me where your great strength comes from, and what would be needed to bind you and tame you."

Samson replied readily enough. "If I were bound with seven green twigs I would lose my strength and become like any other man."

Delilah betrayed Samson to the Philistines who brought seven green twigs and bound Samson while he slept. Then Delilah cried out: "The Philistines are on you, Samson!"

But Samson snapped the twigs as easily as if they had been burnt with fire. So the secret of his strength was still not known. Delilah knew that Samson had tricked her, but she tried again to discover his secret.

And this time Samson said: "If they bind me with new ropes that have never been used before I would lose my strength and become like any other man."

While Samson slept Delilah bound him with new ropes. She had men hidden in the room and she called again: "The Philistines are on you, Samson!"

But Samson snapped the ropes around his arms like thread.

Again Delilah begged Samson to tell her the secret of his strength. "Until now you have been laughing at me and telling me lies. What do I need to really bind you?"

He answered: "If you wove seven strands of my hair into a web and fixed the web firmly into a peg I would lose my strength and become as any other man."

Delilah lulled Samson to sleep and did what he said and called: "The Philistines are on you, Samson!"

Samson woke from sleep and pulled out both the web of hair and the peg which fastened it.

Delilah again begged Samson: "How can you say you love me? Three times have I asked you the same question and three times you have fooled me." Day after day she persisted with her questions until Samson grew weary and tired to death of her begging.

At last he told her his great secret "If my hair is cut off," he said, "my power would forsake me, I would lose my strength and become like any other man."

Delilah was now sure that she had the truth. She waited until Samson was asleep, then she cut off the seven locks of his hair. She cried again: "The Philistines are on you, O Samson!"

Samson rose, expecting to be as strong as before, but he was weak and helpless.

The Philistines bound the powerless Samson and Delilah was paid her money. So that he could do no more harm they put out his eyes and set him to work grinding corn, like any other slave.

But the hair that had been shorn off began to grow again.

One day when the Philistines were having a great feast they sent for Samson to amuse them. As Samson, sightless, was being led into the temple court by a lad, he said: "Lead me to where I can touch the pillars on which the house stands, so that I may lean against one of them."

All the Philistine chiefs were there, as well as three thousand men and women. Samson, grasping the two middle pillars that supported the building, threw his entire weight against them, his right arm against one and his left arm against the other. Then with a prayer of vengeance he thrust with all his might, calling out: "May I die with the Philistines!"

Bowing forward he pulled the pillars over with him. The house fell on

Samson, the chiefs and all the people there. Those Philistines who Samson killed at his death outnumbered all those he had killed during his lifetime. For many years afterwards the Philistines did not oppress the Israelites.

The tribes of Israel were eventually able to unite sufficiently to fight off the Philistines until the end of the eleventh century B.C., when they suffered a crushing defeat. This humiliation prompted them to look for a king, like the other nations around them. The people reasoned that a leader such as a king would lead them out of their troubles and into a more successful role.

Saul was the first king to rule the united tribes of Israel. He reigned from about 1025–1004 B.C. He built up an army to fight the Philistines; it was in one of their encounters that the young shepherd David killed the Philistine warrior-giant, Goliath. King David, then Solomon, ruled over Israel, and Jerusalem became the centre of government and worship.

After Solomon's death the kingdom was split by internal conflict into the kingdoms of Israel and Judah. Only when they were threatened by the Assyrians did they join forces again. But in 732 B.C. Tiglath Pileser III, king of Assyria, defeated them all, and the Israelites were sent into exile in distant provinces.

As the strength of Assyria waned King Josiah of Judah reclaimed some of the territory and repaired the Holy Temple in Jerusalem. However the Babylonian King Nebuchadnezzar invaded Judea and in 586 B.C. he sacked the Temple and exiled most of the Jewish people. This period in Jewish history is known as The Captivity.

When Cyrus, king of Persia, conquered Babylonia in 539 B.C. he permitted the Jews to return to Jerusalem and rebuild their Temple. In 458 B.C. the prophet Ezra led several thousand Jews to Jerusalem. The Persians allowed the Jews freedom of worship; this was continued under the rule of Alexander the Great, king of Macedonia, who was the next conqueror of their land.

After Alexander came the Ptolemies from Egypt; then the Seleucids from Syria. For a short time the kingdom of Judah achieved independence under John Hyrcanus, from 134–104 B.C. But constant bickering weakened the claim of the Jews. In 63 B.C. Pompey, the Roman commander, invaded Jerusalem and the land of Israel became part of the Roman Empire.

Old England

British myth and legend combines three traditions: the Celtic, the Viking and the Norman. The Celts were the ancestors of most modern Europeans. By about 300 B.C. these Indo-Europeans ruled from the Baltic to the Mediterranean seas, and from the Black Sea to Ireland. The earliest civilisation in Britain was Celtic and even today Celtic place names, superstitions and festivals survive in Ireland, much of Scotland, Wales, Cornwall and the Isle of Man.

In Celtic society the Druids were the priests and scholars and were concerned with the worship of the gods, the law, science and magic. They passed down by word of mouth stories of their gods, goddesses, heroes and heroines. Knights comprised the courtly class and went into battle, while the common people were little more than slaves.

Irish literature records the earliest myths of the Irish Celts — the four invasions of Ireland including that of the Tuatha de Danann, the children of Danu, and the old gods of Ireland. In addition to their gods the Irish had their heroes, and the greatest of them was Cuchulain.

From Wales comes *The Mabinogion*, a collection of oral tales written down in medieval times. The most frequently told is that of the hero Pryderi, son of Pwyll, Prince of Dyfed. This tale is divided into four parts or "branches" and tells of Pryderi's wondrous birth and childhood, his great exploits, his brave deeds, his courtship, his misfortunes and his death.

The famed King Arthur appears in some of the tales of *The Mabinogion*; the original Arthur is thought by some to have been a Celtic chieftain and by others a pagan Celtic god.

118

Although the character of Arthur exists from Celtic times, his image as we now have it was largely created by Geoffrey of Monmouth in 1135. It was Geoffrey who gave Arthur his heroic stature, relating his history to the Greek heroes but also placing him in the Christian tradition. So the Arthur story is part Celtic, part medieval Norman and part Christian.

Before the coming of the Normans, England was invaded by Northmen who came from the area we now know as Scandinavia. They also brought with them stories of their great heroes. It is possible that the story of Beowulf is derived from stories of the valorous nephew of Hygelac—a Norse chief who led a plundering expedition up the Rhine, and who saved remnants of his uncle's army by a marvellous feat of swimming. Others believe that the events which provide the basis for the story of Beowulf took place on English soil. Still others see in the ending of Beowulf an image of the generosity of King Arthur. Certain it is that when the great poem was written there existed various northern legends of Beowa, a half-divine hero, and the monster Grendel.

Throughout Britain tales are still told of great heroes of the past. Some of them are Celtic in origin, some Anglo-Saxon and others have assumed the trappings of a medieval knight in the European tradition.

Beowulf the Dragon Slayer

One of the earliest of English heroes is Beowulf, a warrior whose exploits form the basis of a 30,000-line epic poem written by an unknown poet in Old English. The manuscript, which is kept in the British Museum, dates back to before A.D. 1000, but the poem existed orally among the Anglo-Saxon people long before that, possibly as far back as the fifth century.

Of Beowulf's birth we know nothing and the epic tells little of the early life of this heroic monster-slayer. We do know that he was a nephew of King Hygelac who ruled an ancient Swedish tribe called the Geats. When he was but a boy Beowulf and his fellow page, Breca, made a bargain to see how long they could swim together in the open sea. They each carried an unsheathed sword to defend themselves against sharks and sea monsters. Although Beowulf was faster than his young friend they stayed together for five nights until a fierce wind and a tempestuous sea drove them apart. Pounding waves stirred strange creatures of the deeps to fury. One huge spotted monster took hold of Beowulf and dragged him to the bed of the ocean, still clad in his golden corselet and hand-linked coat of mail. With a tremendous effort Beowulf drove upward with his sword and ran his attacker through the heart. Almost immediately another creature attacked and once again Beowulf thrust his sword to dispatch it. The battle raged throughout the night and when the waves grew calmer and the sun shone in the east as a beacon from God, nine monsters of the deep were tossed up on to the shore, nevermore to destroy passing ships or unwary seamen.

Beowulf grew into a hero with the heart of a lion and the strength of thirty men in his arms. How he fought the monster Grendel is one of England's most stirring legends.

In the far-off days when Hrothgar was king of Denmark, a monster-dragon called Grendel terrorised the countryside. Rising from the marshy fens Grendel

stalked through the night, even to the hall of the King, where he was known to seize as many as thirty of Hrothgar's sleeping warriors and devour them. Gathering fifteen more into his hideous arms he would carry them off to his lair.

For twelve years this slaughter continued until the great hall became derelict and deserted. Still the demon, descendant of Cain, marauded the countryside like the very shadow of death, plotting against young and old. No night was ever safe on the fog-bound moors of Denmark. Hrothgar lived constantly with this trouble heavy on his heart.

News of this reign of terror spread far and wide, and reached the land of the Geats where the hero Beowulf dwelt. He was said to be the strongest man alive, fearless and bold. It was he who ordered a ship to be equipped and provisioned, then announced that he would cross the sea to Denmark and lend his aid to the harassed King. He chose fourteen of the bravest warriors to go with him and when the omens were favourable he led the way to the shore and set sail.

The curved prow of the ship darted like a bird over the water and on the second day the voyagers made landfall and accosted the coast-guard, who led the party to the King's high hall . . .

Beowulf slays Grendel

While Beowulf and his band were waiting within the sad old walls of Heorot, the hall of the King, a venerable chieftain called Wulfgar approached and asked, "From where have you come with your gold-plated shields, your mail corselets and your great stack of iron-headed spears? Never in my life have I seen such equipment or such stalwart warriors. I am Hrothgar's chief-officer and must know your mission."

Then the helmeted leader stepped forward and spoke in clear, ringing tones: "My name is Beowulf and we come from Hygelac, ruler of the Geats. I shall explain our mission to the King himself if he will grant us audience."

Wulfgar hastened to where the King sat bowed with grief.

"A party of Geats whose leader is called Beowulf begs audience, my lord. They come fully armed but are courteous. They look to be men of courage and valour. I pray you, sir, receive them well."

The weary King rose to his feet and stepped forward. "This young man, I know him well from when he was but a lad. Now he has grown to manhood and I hear tell that in his hand-grip he has the strength of thirty men. Surely God has sent him to our aid against the terror of Grendel. Bid him and his men welcome and bring them into my presence with honour."

Wulfgar lost no time ushering the band and their leader into the royal presence. With quick steps the Geats, a fine body of men, led by Beowulf, marched under the rafters of Heorot. The hero himself, a commanding figure in his gleaming corselet of fine chain-mail, advanced to the foot of the throne. With a steady look and utter assurance Beowulf spoke:

"Hail to you Hrothgar, king of the Danes. I am King Hygelac's nephew and his thane. Seafaring men have come to our land with pitiful tales of plunder and pillage, of the scourge on your lord's domain brought about by the demon Grendel. So we have come, O royal Hrothgar, to aid you. In my youth I won renown for my mighty and valorous deeds. My countrymen have urged me to visit you because they know my strength and power. Already I have slain a whole family of giants, capturing five of them alive, and at night I have destroyed many a monster of the sea. Many a time I have been battered in combat, but never beaten. As I have helped preserve the safety of the Geats so now I come to fight single-handed the monstrous devil Grendel.

"But, my lord, one petition I have of you. I hear tell that this demon in his boastfulness despises the use of weapons. So I shall dispense with both my shield and my sword. I shall meet the monster, foe to foe, and fight the fiend to the death with only my bare hands. Whichever of us is vanquished, it will be the will of God.

"Should that one be me," continued Beowulf, "do not go to the expense of burying me, for the monster will eat my remains, bearing off my bloody corpse to his marshy moor. He will stain the swamps with my blood and the blood of my followers. So should I be killed by Grendel I ask only that you send to my uncle Hygelac the coat of mail that protects me, for it is the best corselet ever made, having been fashioned by the most skilled of smiths. It is an heirloom bequeathed to me by my grandfather so it must be returned to my family. But God will decide my fate."

To this manly and noble speech the aged King made a long but dignified reply. He, too, spoke of the exploits and the happiness of his youth. Then he dwelt on the sorrows and disasters of his latter years, when the ravages of Grendel stained the hall of Heorot with carnage and banqueting benches were red with blood.

"But now, you and your followers must sit at banquet with me. Let us share a feast together, and may your confidence in victory be well founded."

As the company feasted, music and song filled the gloomy hall which seemed to take on new life from these lusty visitors from across the sea. A hush fell over the company as Hrothgar's consort, the gracious and lovely Queen Wealhtheow, entered the hall wearing her diadem and finely attired in gold cloth to honour her husband's guests. First she offered a jewelled goblet of wine to her husband and then, exchanging gracious words of greeting, she visited each corner of the hall from elder to younger until she came to Beowulf himself. As she proffered him the goblet she said, "I thank God for your coming and I pray that with his aid you will accomplish what you have come to do."

"Dear lady," replied the hero, "God has sped me and my men across the waters to your land, which I have vowed to deliver from the forces of evil. He will be by my side."

The Queen inclined her diademed head, well pleased with what he said, then took her place at her husband's side.

The feasting continued well into the day until the King, knowing that when daylight fled and the shrouds of night descended the monster would creep from its lair, rose to his feet. Song and laughter died away.

"Never since I was able to bear arms have I entrusted the guard-house of the Danes to any man. So, Beowulf, have and hold my ancestral hall; be watchful and vigilant. Remember your reputation, take pride in your strength. No wish of yours will remain unfulfilled if you live through this great undertaking." So spoke the king of the Danes, then slowly he left the hall with the Queen on his arm.

Beowulf, confident in his strength and the favour of God, took off his shining steel corselet, laid aside his helmet and gave his patterned sword to his attendant, ordering him to take charge of his armour.

"Not against Grendel shall I wield my sword. Tonight I shall fight him with my bare hands. May God give me the victory."

The hall was now cleared of its benches and couches were made of pelts and rugs as the Geats followed their leader's example and laid themselves down to rest. Gradually weariness from their journey and the excitement of the feasting overtook them and one by one they fell into sleep — except for Beowulf who lay still, his ears straining and his eyes peering into the gloom.

Minutes passed, then hours. The men turned in their sleep while Beowulf kept his lonely vigil.

But from the marshes the prowler came stalking. Through the mists that rose from the bogs and by the light of the rent in the clouds it prowled in search of human flesh. At the entrance of the banqueting hall, its gold-plated door fastened with bars of iron, the monster paused. It was not the first time it had visited Heorot. With malicious fury it tore at the door with its talons and with eyes ablaze he stepped on to the tessellated floor.

At the sight of the sleeping warriors Grendel laughed hideously. Before daylight he would have them, every one. Still Beowulf watched, waiting to see how the demon would act.

The fiend acted swiftly. With one movement he snatched up a sleeping warrior, tore him apart, drank the blood from his veins and devoured the man in

great gulps, feet and hands and everything.

Then it turned in Beowulf's direction and lunged at the hero. But Beowulf was faster than the monster. In a moment he gripped the fiend in his bare hands. Never before had the son of Cain felt a grip like Beowulf's. Rid himself of this vice-like grip he must. In deathly fear he thrashed about in an effort to free himself and flee back to his hiding place in the stinking marshes. But his talons were held fast in a superhuman clutch. The great hall thundered with the din of the combat. The company of the Geats watched with horror. Outside the Danes stood petrified by the hubbub. The building shook as man and demon locked in mortal combat. Benches decorated with inlaid gold were uprooted and over-turned, and only the strength of the iron stanchions inside and out kept the building intact. Still the wrestlers writhed until the earth shook, the waves dashed madly at the shore and the skies seemed to tremble.

Many of Beowulf's men drew their swords ready to defend their leader. Little did they know that the fiend had cast such powerful spells that no blade on earth could destroy it. But even such a spell would not hold out against the invincibility of the human spirit and the forces of right which were to prevail.

Beowulf had Grendel by the claw and the demon was shot through with excruciating pain. A gaping wound extended from his shoulder, as sinews strained and snapped, tendons burst asunder and Beowulf wrenched the horrible arm from its socket. The monster, knowing that the wound was fatal and his time had run out, shambled away to its foul lair on the fens, there to sink into the gloomy depths of the lake now boiling with the blood of the demon.

So Beowulf's bravery, his faith in himself and the justice of his cause emerged intact. Heorot was purged of the evil that was Grendel; as a sign, Beowulf hung the monster's claw-like limb from the gabled roof of the hall.

Chieftains came from far and near to rejoice at their delivery from the pestilence of Grendel. Throughout the day the air was filled with songs of praise and rejoicing; feasting was interrupted only by horse-races, wrestling and other contests of skill and endurance.

King Hrothgar himself, with Queen Wealhtheow on his arm, came to gaze with horror at the dreadful trophy hanging from the gable. Turning to Beowulf the King exclaimed, "Thanks be to the Almighty Father for this happy sight! Years of sorrow and distress have I endured at the hands of Grendel, many warriors have I lost, much pain has been inflicted on my subjects, but God, the king of glory, has performed a miracle. A youth has, in the strength of the Lord, achieved what all our schemes could not accomplish. Beowulf, exult in your fame! A son in love you shall be to me henceforth. Nothing that you desire shall not be given you if it is in my power to do so. Many times have I rewarded less heroic deeds with great gifts, so to you I can deny nothing."

To this Beowulf replied, "I have fulfilled my boast, and driven away your enemy. Would that I could have left him dead in this hall, but God did not will it so. The fiend was too quick for me, but his claw, his arm and his shoulder remain here as a token of his evil presence and as the ransom price of his loathsome body which will live no longer. The demon must now wait the last judgement and the sentence of Almighty God."

Then the hall was cleared of all traces of the battle, a banquet was prepared and joy flooded like sunlight through Heorot. The walls were hung with tapestries of embroidered gold and expensive cloth, goblets shone with the lustre of victory and the exploits of the night were recounted over and over again.

Beowulf and King Hrothgar sat on the high seats facing one another. Their followers, both Danes and Geats, sat side by side shouting and cheering as they drank to the heroes of the past and the now-famous Beowulf.

Then the King rewarded every man of Beowulf's band and presented the hero with a banner embroidered with gold, a handsome sword, a helmet and corselet, a golden goblet and eight fleet steeds.

After the gifts had been bestowed the Queen arose and lifted her drinking-cup. Turning to Beowulf she said: "Enjoy your reward while you can, noble and blessed Beowulf. Live fast in your fame and should a time of need ever come, be a protector to my sons." She presented him with two jewelled, golden armbands, costly rings, a corselet of fine chain-mail and a collar studded with precious stones of ancient and exquisite workmanship. Then she and her ladies left the hall.

The feast continued until Hrothgar also went his way. Then Beowulf and the Geats were bedded in a nearby lodging and settled to sleep, happy in the knowledge of a mission accomplished with honour.

Grendel's mother and the death of Beowulf

During that night the mother of Grendel, a fiend no less terrible and horrible than her son, came to avenge his death. She burst into the hall and seized Hrothgar's chief counsellor and bore him off into the night, taking also the prized arm of Grendel.

Next morning the Danes woke Beowulf with the news. He and King Hrothgar led a procession to the marshes, where they found the waters stained with blood and the head of the King's counsellor on the bank.

Beowulf immediately prepared to dive down to the monster's lair. When he entered the waters he was beset by hideous creatures until he came at last to where Grendel's awful mother lay in wait.

The sea-woman flung Beowulf on to his back and stabbed at him with the point of her broad knife; only Beowulf's corselet saved him in this almost superhuman contest. The sword he carried was of no avail against her charmed hide, so he engaged the monster in a grim hand-to-hand battle. As he felt his strength failing he caught sight of the famous sword of the giants, an heirloom of heroes which Grendel's mother had captured from some previous victim and now displayed on her wall. He snatched the ancient sword and now used it against its captor to send her to her death.

As the carcass of his foe sank in the mire Beowulf caught sight of Grendel himself, lying dead in an inner hall. Quickly he severed the head from the body and swam upward with the trophy; but before he reached the surface of the marsh the blade of the sword that he still held in his hand melted until only the head and hilt were left. These he presented to Hrothgar after once again being feted. Then Beowulf sailed in glory back to his homeland.

Many years later Beowulf himself became king of the Geats. In the fiftieth year of his reign a monstrous fire-dragon terrorised his lands in revenge for having been robbed of the treasure it guarded. Its blazing breath burned down houses and homesteads and consumed men and cattle with fiery flames from its mouth.

When Beowulf learned of his people's suffering he went to their aid, even though he was now an old man. But he knew that he would never be able to come to hand-grips with the dragon as he had done with Grendel and his mother.

With streams of fiery breath rushing from its nostrils the beast flew at Beowulf whose sword flashed in the able hands of its master, but to no avail. The cowardly Geats fled in dismay except for a warrior named Wiglaf who sprang to the aid of his king. Wiglaf lifted high his wooden shield, which the dragon annihilated as though it were straw. The two warriors then sheltered behind Beowulf's iron shield, but the armour they wore became a torture because of the heat. Then Beowulf struck with his sword but it splintered into fragments against the monster's skull. The enraged dragon flew at Beowulf and seized his neck with its poisonous fangs. Wiglaf, filled with grief and horror, plunged his already shortened sword into the dragon's belly, and Beowulf with his war-knife delivered the final and fatal blow.

Weak now with loss of blood, and poisoned with the brute's venom, the ancient hero lay dying. As Wiglaf bathed his brow with water from a nearby stream the King raised himself a little and, before he died, he asked his loyal friend to unearth the treasure which the dragon had gathered in his lair so that he could view it and be glad in his nation's wealth before he died. When he saw the glorious treasure-hoard the dying King thanked God for the wealth that he was permitted to win for his people in his last moments.

He unclasped the golden collar from his neck, gave it, with his golden helmet, corselet and ring, to the trusty Wiglaf, and died.

The other warriors now came from their hiding places and, though grieving bitterly, at Wiglaf's command they ransacked the dragon's den of its treasure and threw the body of the dead monster over the cliff into the sea.

Beowulf's body was carried on a bier hung with shields and solemnly laid on a vast funeral pyre, where it was ceremoniously burnt to ashes. Upon the headland the Geats erected for their dead ruler a broad, high cairn that would be plainly visible to passing seamen. It took ten days to build the hero's monument and in that barrow they placed the ashes of the King along with the necklets, rings and brooches of the dragon's treasure-trove, where it remains to this day—as useless now as it was when guarded by the dragon.

King Arthur: The Stuff of Heroes

Of all the British heroes, Arthur is the greatest — the most mysterious, the most romantic, the most intriguing. He is a man, a knight, a lover and a ruler. He is also, in part, supernatural man — a visionary for whom the Holy Grail remains a symbol of all that is noble, good and pure.

Ever since Geoffrey of Monmouth, a popular historian of the mid-twelfth century, romanticised the existing legends of a pagan warrior in his *History of the Kings of Britain*, Arthur, his bride Guinevere, his Knights of the Round Table and the fabled court of Camelot have fired the imagination of poets, artists, musicians, song-writers and writers for the stage and film.

In actuality it is likely that there did exist a Celtic chieftain, called Artos, possibly a cavalry leader. When the Romans withdrew their garrisons from Britain in the fifth century, Artos rallied his people against the Saxon invaders and after a number of battles defeated the Saxons decisively at Mount Badon in about A.D. 516. Although Cornwall claims him as a son this leader seems to have ranged widely throughout Britain. Two of the Scilly Isles are called Great and Little Arthur, a hill near Edinburgh is called Arthur's Seat, and many other places bear his name.

The figure of this chivalrous yet successful leader could well have taken on something of the mystique of the pagan Celtic god called Artor. Certain it is that from the time of Geoffrey of Monmouth legendary stories of King Arthur multiplied and spread throughout Britain and Europe, even to Italy. In 1155 a Norman poet called Robert Wace added the story of the Round Table to Geoffrey of Monmouth's history. He suggested that Arthur thought of a round table so that no one knight would seem to be more important than another — all would be equal in this circle of friendship.

Later in the same century a French poet, Chrétien de Troyes, was but one writer to add many new stories to the Arthurian cycle: the love stories of Lancelot and Guinevere, Tristan and Iseult; Sir Galahad's quest for the Holy Grail; and the story of Camelot itself.

Throughout the thirteenth, fourteenth and fifteenth centuries numerous romances in both verse and prose were written in English, but it was Sir Thomas Malory who wrote the famous collection of Arthur stories now known as *Le Morte d'Arthur*, printed in 1485 by William Caxton. From Malory's tales of the golden age of chivalry come a host of Arthurian exploits. Even today writers are fascinated by the heroic Arthur, and elements from Geoffrey of Monmouth, Chrétien de Troyes, Thomas Malory and other unnamed writers provide the basis for contemporary fantasy, and literary hero-tales of this man King Arthur.

The birth of Arthur

In those far-off days when Uther Pendragon was king over all England, there was a duke of Tintagel who rebelled against the King's power, continually challenging him in a series of battles. At length Uther persuaded the Duke to call a halt to hostilities and invite both the Duke and his wife, the lovely Igraine, to a meeting of reconciliation.

No sooner had the powerful King looked on Igraine than he fell in love with her and wanted her for his own. But Igraine was loyal to her husband and refused the King's advances. So incensed was she that she convinced the Duke that they should flee the palace together and return to Tintagel.

When Uther discovered the couple's flight he was furious and sent messengers to say that unless they returned immediately he would send an army to bring them back. Instead of obeying Uther, the Duke left Igraine in the safety of the fortified castle at Tintagel and shut himself up with an army at another castle called Terrabil, to which King Uther immediately laid siege. Many battles followed and many men from both sides were slain.

Yet even while the fighting raged the King continued to think so fervently about Igraine that he fell sick with love for her, to the dismay and anger of his knights. In fear for themselves as well as their King a council of the knights sent for Merlin the wizard. It was said that Merlin could not only see into the future, but could cast magic spells and even change his own shape and appearance. While yet a boy he had become the king's chief counsellor because of his great wisdom and powerful gifts of magic.

131

The knight who was sent to fetch Merlin hadn't gone far before he met a decrepit-looking beggar who approached him saying, "I am he for whom you seek, and I know the desire of your master's heart. And he shall have whatever he wishes provided he rewards me well."

"My master, the King, is powerful enough to grant whatever you want—as well you know," replied the knight, and together they entered the King's presence.

"You don't have to tell me, Uther, what is in your heart," said the beggar. "Well I know it. And you shall have it. But, first, promise on your oath as King that you shall do as I demand."

"So be it," replied the King and swore solemnly that Merlin should have whatever he asked.

"Then you shall have Igraine. Also she will bear you a son, but that son you must give to me to keep—for the sake of your honour and for the child's good."

"That I promise," vowed the King.

"Then come with me to the castle of Tintagel," said the wizard.

No sooner had Merlin and Uther slipped away from the King's pavilion outside the castle walls than Merlin cast a spell and changed Uther into the likeness of the Duke.

But the real Duke had seen, from the castle ramparts, the King and the beggar riding off. It was then that he decided to attack the besieging army. Soon after nightfall he led the charge, only to fall dead from the arrow of one of Uther's bowmen.

So it was that Uther, in the shape of the Duke, arrived at Tintagel and went in to the lady Igraine who imagined that it was her husband returned to her, although that night he said but little except to proclaim his love. The next morning he left her. Not long after, messengers brought news of the Duke's death. Igraine immediately realised that she had been deceived, but wisely kept her counsel and decided to wait in silence, although sorely grieved by the loss of her husband.

With the Duke dead and his army defeated Uther was indeed the undisputed king of England and claimed Igraine as his bride who, on the advice of her counsellors, accepted him. They were married with royal ceremony and Igraine saw that the King loved her truly.

When her son was born Uther confessed to Igraine that he had tricked her and that he was in truth the father of her child. He told her, too, of the pact that he had made with Merlin who now claimed his part of the bargain, promising that the child should come to no harm but rather that his name should become known throughout the land.

So, still in his beggar's garb, Merlin took the unchristened child and wrapped it

in a cloak embroidered with gold; and the King was never to see his son again. But Merlin took the babe to a devout and honourable knight called Sir Ector who had him christened Arthur and who, with his wife, brought up the child as a son, but also as a prince.

Some years passed and King Uther fell sorely ill and it became clear that he had not long to live, even while hostile armies from the north were invading the land.

Merlin approached the stricken monarch. "My lord, you must lead your men to battle if you wish to destroy the enemy. Your presence on the field will embolden and give new heart to your men."

As ill as he was the King did what Merlin suggested and a great battle was waged at St. Albans, and the invaders were routed. All of London rejoiced, but rejoicing turned to sorrow when it was learned that the King was dying.

Once more Merlin approached the King, but in private. "My Lord, who is to succeed you on the throne of England?"

The King looked sadly at Merlin, silently asking his advice and help for the last time.

"Is your son, Arthur, to be your heir and rule England?"

Then Uther Pendragon raised himself and said, "Arthur has my blessing. May he wear the crown with honour, reign justly and wisely . . . and may he remember me with love." And the king of England died.

The sword in the stone

When King Uther died the people believed that he had left no son to rule because the birth of Arthur had been kept secret, even though many years before Merlin had prophesied that after Uther there would come a far greater king than he, his son Arthur.

Only Merlin knew the secret of Arthur's birth and that he was destined to become king. Not even Sir Ector knew of the boy's true parentage but brought him up as his own son, proud and pleased as the boy grew tall and handsome and accomplished in all knightly tasks and chivalrous pursuits.

But because no one knew of Arthur's whereabouts, even though it was rumoured that the King had named an heir, many powerful lords and nobles began to fight among themselves for the crown, each believing he should be ruler of England. Civil war seemed almost inevitable. While the nobles fought among themselves great evils fell upon the land and invaders came from across the sea to pillage and plunder.

So the Archbishop, advised by Merlin, sent for all the lords and gentlemen of arms to come to London by Christmas for a tourney. "Come to London, and God will show us who is the true and rightful king," he decreed.

When the nobles assembled in London and attended the great church there, they saw in the churchyard, against the high altar, a huge stone. Into the middle of this stone was wedged an anvil of steel a foot high, and in this anvil was embedded a naked sword. Engraved on the sword in letters of gold were the words, "Whoso pulleth this sword out of this stone and anvil, is rightly born king of Britain".

Immediately many of the nobles and knights of the realm who wished to be king tried to draw the sword, but none could even stir it. So the Archbishop decreed that every man who so wished should be allowed to try to win the sword, but that ten men of good repute should keep watch by it.

On New Year's Day, when the service was over, the barons and knights rode into the field, some to joust and some to tourney. It so happened that Sir Ector rode to the joust and with him his son, Sir Kay, and young Arthur as his squire. As they rode Sir Kay discovered that he had left his sword at his father's lodging and he asked Arthur to fetch it for him.

Arthur hastened to do as Sir Kay had requested but when he arrived at the inn, the door was locked and everyone had gone to the jousting. Arthur was angry and said to himself, "I will ride to the churchyard and take the sword that is wedged in the anvil, for my brother, Sir Kay, must not be without a sword today."

When he came to the churchyard, young Arthur dismounted from his horse and went to the tent where the knights were to be keeping watch. But they were all away at the jousting. So he strode to where the sword gleamed in the sunlight, took it by the handle and gave it a great pull. The sword came away immediately. Then Arthur mounted his horse, rode back to Sir Kay and delivered him the sword.

As soon as Sir Kay saw the sword, he knew which it was and rode immediately to his father crying, "Sir, here is the sword out of the stone. Therefore I must be king of Britain."

Sir Ector immediately hurried Sir Kay and Arthur back to the churchyard and there he demanded that Sir Kay swear on a book how he came by the sword.

"Sir," replied Sir Kay, "by my brother Arthur, for he brought the sword to me."

"How came you by this sword?" Sir Ector challenged Arthur.

"I drew it from the anvil in the stone so that Sir Kay should have a sword."

"Were you seen by any man?"

"No my lord, there was no one to see me."

"Then," said Sir Ector, "I understand you must be king of this land. But first, let me see if I can return the sword to the stone, as it was before, and you pull it out again."

"That is no difficult matter," said Arthur. Thereupon Sir Ector thrust the sword back into the stone.

"Now try to withdraw the sword," said Sir Ector to his son, Sir Kay. But Sir Kay could not.

The old man turned to Arthur. "Now it is your turn."

So Arthur tried, and pulled the sword out easily. Upon that, Sir Ector and Sir Kay kneeled before the boy.

"My lord and my king," said Sir Ector. "You are no son of mine, but now I know whose son you are!"

Then they went to the Archbishop and told him how the sword had been won and by whom. Even then many of the barons and knights were angry and tried again to draw the sword from the stone. But none succeeded. Only Arthur was able to free the sword.

Thereupon the people of the land cried out, "We will have Arthur for our king and let there be no more delay."

It was only then that Merlin came forward to tell the lords and barons that their chosen king was the true son of their beloved Uther Pendragon and that Sir Ector had raised the lad in trust for the King. Although Arthur was sad to lose Sir Ector as a father, he knew that he would have him as a friend and counsellor.

So he laid the wondrous sword from the stone across his outstretched hands and placed it upon the altar of the church. He swore to be a true king as his father had wished; to stand always for justice, truth and honour and to rule his people wisely. That day the Archbishop made Arthur a knight, then crowned him king of Britain; and all the barons, knights and squires paid homage to their new king, swearing to serve and obey him in all things.

So began a long and splendid reign filled with wonderful deeds and exploits, the like of which have never again been heard, in Britain or in any land.

The last days and the death of Arthur

When the sword from the stone was shattered in a fight Merlin took Arthur to a magic lake. From the centre of this lake rose an arm clothed in white samite and holding a gleaming sword whose golden hilt was studded with jewels, a jewelled scabbard and a belt.

A beautiful maiden, calling herself the Lady of the Lake, approached Arthur and offered him the sword, which she called Excalibur, as a gift. Then the lady summoned a miraculous barge which bore the King across the lake to the arm, which extended the sword and its scabbard to Arthur, then sank between the blue waters. When Arthur returned to the shore, the lady had vanished.

Arthur buckled on the sword Excalibur and Merlin told him to guard well the scabbard, for its power would always protect the King, no matter how grievously he was wounded.

Soon, Arthur was to marry the beautiful Guinevere, set up court in Camelot, and establish the Order of the Round Table — that order of knights who vowed to live nobly and fight valiantly. Many stories are told of these famous knights — Lancelot, Galahad, Tristan, Gareth, Percival and many more; but perhaps the finest and bravest of them all was Sir Gawain.

Arthur's glory and popularity grew as his enemies were subdued but the years of peace did not last and his later days were filled with great sadness. Knights who rode out in search of the Holy Grail, said to be the vessel which Christ used at the Last Supper, failed to return. Arthur's bravest knight and best friend, Sir Lancelot, sometimes known as Lancelot of the Lake, fell in love with Arthur's wife, Queen Guinevere. Although the couple tried to keep their love secret there were those who were jealous of the favours the Queen bestowed upon Sir Lancelot. It was Arthur's nephew, the traitorous Sir Mordred, who eventually brought shame and ruin not only upon the Queen and Sir Lancelot, but who destroyed Arthur himself. Merlin had warned about the trouble Mordred would bring.

When Sir Mordred overheard the Queen and Sir Lancelot arranging to meet in secret, he gloated in the darkness. That night he and twelve knights burst into the Queen's chamber while Sir Lancelot was with her and accused them both of treachery to the King. Sir Lancelot met his accusers with a flashing sword and killed them all but Sir Mordred, whom he wounded. Then Sir Lancelot fled Camelot and hid in the nearby forest, waiting to see what would happen.

But Sir Mordred, wounded, went directly to Arthur to lay charges of treason against Lancelot and Guinevere. With the King dishonoured, he planned to stir up civil war and seize the throne for himself. When Arthur heard Mordred's sorry story the King knew that the fellowship of the Round Table had come to an end, and that his own happiness was over. With great sorrow he pronounced Sir Lancelot an outlaw and condemned the Queen to death by burning, according to the law.

So on the appointed day the lady Guinevere, dressed only in a flowing robe, was led to the stake. Just as the burning brand was about to be thrust into the pyre Sir Lancelot, who had sworn to save Guinevere whatever the cost, swooped with his men like lightning and freed the Queen, slaying many of the knights who were carrying out the King's command. Sir Lancelot and Queen Guinevere escaped to Sir Lancelot's castle in France so that Arthur was forced by his honour to follow them, leaving the treacherous Sir Mordred behind to rule in England.

This was Mordred's opportunity to usurp the King's position and seize the crown for himself. As soon as news of this betrayal was brought to Arthur he returned at once to England to do battle with the traitor-knight. There were a series of bloody encounters between the armies of Arthur and the pretender until they met at Camlann in what they both knew must be the last battle — one way or the other. Already the Archbishop of Canterbury, the priest who had crowned Arthur king, had cursed Sir Mordred and put him outside the rites and blessings of the church.

On the eve of the great battle Arthur could not sleep. As he tossed between sleeping and waking he had a vision of the dead knight, Sir Gawain, who came to him with a train of ladies in whose cause he had fought in life. Sir Gawain warned him not to do battle with Sir Mordred. "Call a truce for but a month," begged the ghostly knight, "for if you delay awhile Sir Lancelot and his knights will come to your aid and together you will defeat the usurper." Then Sir Gawain and his ladies vanished, leaving the King sorely perplexed.

When Arthur told his priests of the omen which had come in the night they advised him to arrange the truce as the ghost of Sir Gawain had suggested.

So a truce was agreed upon. It was arranged that Arthur and Sir Mordred, each accompanied by fourteen knights, would meet at a spot between the two armies. Because Arthur could not trust Mordred he gave an order to his men. "If you see a drawn sword, come swiftly and kill the traitor Sir Mordred, for I fear his treachery." While he was speaking Sir Mordred was addressing his knights, "If you see a drawn sword, come swiftly and kill every one of Arthur's men, for I do not trust the King who has sworn vengeance upon us all."

Then the parties advanced into the middle ground, the treaty was drawn up and signed, and wine was passed around as a token of good faith. Even as they were drinking an adder slid from the grass and stung one of Sir Mordred's knights on the heel. Without thinking he drew his sword to kill it and as he did so the blade caught the sunlight so that both watching armies saw its gleam.

Battle cries were shouted as both armies attacked. All day long the battle raged until the plain of Camlann was strewn with corpses. King Arthur wept to see the carnage. Only two of his knights, Sir Lucan and Sir Bedivere, survived, and they both were wounded.

As he looked in sorrow around the battlefield he saw Sir Mordred leaning on his sword amid a heap of bodies. "Give me my spear that I may rid the world of this traitor," called Arthur to Sir Lucan.

"Nay, my lord; remember Sir Gawain's warning. Mordred is already under a curse. Let him be," replied Sir Lucan.

"Never!" shouted Arthur, and sprang at his enemy, calling, "Now, traitor, your death is upon you!" He plunged his spear deep into Sir Mordred's body. Knowing that he had received his death-wound Sir Mordred made a final effort and swung his sword, cutting through Arthur's helmet into the royal head, before he himself fell screaming to the ground.

But Arthur sank silently to the earth. He was carried by Sir Lucan and Sir Bedivere to a wayside chapel not far from a lake which was bathed in gory light from the setting sun, as though stained with the blood of knights. Soon, the strain of moving the King was too much for Sir Lucan whose wounds were gravely deep, and he too died, leaving only Sir Bedivere to attend the King.

Then King Arthur, hardly able to speak, commanded Sir Bedivere to take his sword Excalibur—the sword which, when he was but a young king, had come to him by an arm from a lake—and cast it into this lake so that it might be returned to the Otherworld from whence it came.

As Sir Bedivere raised his arm to throw the sword his eye was caught by its jewelled hilt. He was so overcome with a sense of loss that he hid the sword in the rushes and returned to the King, telling him that he had done as Arthur had commanded.

"And what did you see?" enquired the King.

"Nothing, Sir, but the wind stirring the waters of the lake," replied the knight.

"Then you do not speak truly," said the King. "Do as I command you and throw Excalibur into the waters of the lake."

Once again Sir Bedivere returned to the lake but could not do the deed, and once again the King questioned him.

A third time—and now sternly—Arthur bade his knight do as he was told. "Would you betray your King for the price of a sword? Do as I bid you, before I die."

This time Sir Bedivere took Excalibur and flung it far out into the depths of the lake. As the sword flashed through the moonlight and plunged downward a long, pale arm reached up from the depths and the hand caught it by the hilt, brandished it in the air three times, then slowly vanished beneath the stillness of the lake. The Lady of the Lake had once again taken possession of her gift.

When Sir Bedivere returned and told Arthur what had happened, the King was satisfied. "Now take me to the shore," he said. And Sir Bedivere did as the King commanded.

When they reached the shore of the silent lake a white barge slid into view. On it were three queens and many ladies, all veiled in black, weeping and moaning at the sight of the wounded, dying King.

"Now place me on the barge," instructed the King.

Sir Bedivere did as he was commanded and the three queens received Arthur with tenderness, and one cradled his head in her lap. Then the barge moved slowly and silently out from the land and Sir Bedivere was left, desolate, on the shore.

"What shall become of me now, Lord Arthur, that you leave me here among my enemies," he cried.

"Comfort yourself," came the King's voice, "and do the best you can, for I am no longer able to help you. I must go to Avalon, there to be healed of my most grievous wounds. If Britain has need of me I will come again. And if you never hear of me again, pray for my soul!"

With these last words a mist descended on the face of the lake and the barge moved beyond view of the human eye, and a sigh of sadness rose from the waters.

Some say that Arthur sleeps still in Avalon, while his wounds heal, awaiting the call to return to the upper world as king in the hour of his country's need. Others say that he sleeps in the fiery cradle of Etna, or at Snowdon in Wales, or at Glastonbury.

Perhaps he rests in the hearts of all noble men.

Hic Iacet Arthurus, Rex Quondam Rex que Futurus — Here lies Arthur, the Once and Future King.

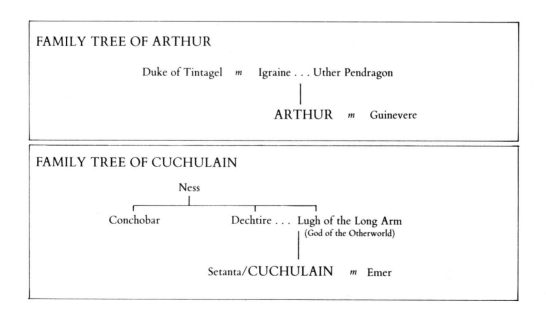

FAMILY TREE OF ARTHUR

Duke of Tintagel *m* Igraine . . . Uther Pendragon

ARTHUR *m* Guinevere

FAMILY TREE OF CUCHULAIN

Ness

Conchobar   Dechtire . . . Lugh of the Long Arm
                              (God of the Otherworld)

Setanta/CUCHULAIN *m* Emer

Cuchulain the Champion

The stories of the great Irish saga, known as the Ulster Cycle, were collected between about 100 B.C. and A.D. 100 and were first written in Celtic Irish. The original Ulster Cycle has been claimed the equal of the *Iliad* and the *Odyssey* in length and brilliance of telling. Certainly it is one of the world's great stories and was given a literary form about the same time as Beowulf.

At the beginning of the twentieth century Lady Gregory, who had learned Old Irish, translated the ancient sagas into the Kiltartan dialect of modern Ireland. Even though the deeds of Cuchulain—the central hero, sometimes known as "the Irish Achilles"—had lived on in the oral stories of the Gaels of Ireland and Scotland, they could now be shared with all who desire to hear of the "great deeds of heroes in their strength".

The birth and naming of Cuchulain

In the long ago time Conchobar, son of Ness, was king of Ulster, and a good time it was for the people of that kingdom. It happened once that Conchobar made a great feast at the palace of Emain Macha for the marriage of his sister Dechtire. During the feast Dechtire accidentally swallowed a mayfly with her wine and immediately fell into a deep sleep. In her sleep Lugh of the Long Arm, the god of the Otherworld, appeared to her and confessed that he was the mayfly and had come to carry away Dechtire and fifty of her maidens to his kingdom.

It was a year later that Bricriu of the Bitter Tongue, one of the chief men of Ulster, was captured and led to a house by a great flock of beautiful birds, flying linked together by chains of silver and gold. At the house, Bricriu was met by a young woman, fine and noble, who gave him a purple cloak fringed with gold to take to Conchobar.

Wrapped in the mysterious cloak, Conchobar went to the house. Arriving, he heard the cry of a child and, upon entering the house, he was amazed to find his sister Dechtire with a young child beside her!

So Conchobar took his sister back to Emain and claimed the child, who was called Setanta, as his nephew. He promised that the boy would learn from the chief men of Ulster. At that time, it was foretold by a wise man that in the years to come the boy would be honoured by chariot-drivers and warriors, by kings and sages and that he would be greatly loved; that he would defend his country, fight for the people and avenge the wrongs done to them.

Setanta was brought up by his mother and her husband in a large house on the Plain of Muirthemne, away from the court at Emain. One day, when he was about seven, he heard people talking about the sons of kings and nobles who lived at the court of King Conchobar and who spent much of their time at warrior games, hurling, and playing a game like football. When he begged and pestered his mother to allow him to go to the court and join in the games she told him to wait until he was older and could travel the distance.

Never one to give up so easily, even at such a young age, Setanta secretly set out then and there with his hurling stick and silver ball, and armed with a homemade shield and a spear. To shorten the journey he would hurl his ball in front of him, race towards it, hurl it again and chase it until eventually he came to the great lawn outside the palace at Emain Macha, where nearly two hundred youths of the nobility were playing warlike games and football.

Without waiting to be invited to join the game the boy from Muirthemne ran in, collected the ball and kicked it well beyond the goal. The other boys were outraged by this insolence from a stranger and attacked him with their hurling sticks, their balls and their spears. Setanta was furious at this injustice and flew at the fellows knocking them easily to the ground.

Conchobar, who was playing chess, heard the commotion and sent for the boy asking what all the fuss was about. "It's a rough game you're playing, lad," he shouted angrily.

"And it's rough they are," replied Setanta. "I came as a stranger and they treated me as an enemy. They deserve what I gave them."

When Conchobar saw that it was his own nephew who spoke out so boldly he took him into the palace at Emain Macha to live, and there the great men of Ulster all had a hand in bringing him up. From then on the other boys were wary of the son of Dechtire who won goals from them all. "That little fellow will serve Ulster yet," said Conchobar as he watched him.

A short time later the King set out in his chariots for a feast laid out in his honour by Culain, a great smith of Ulster. As he passed Setanta playing with his fellows he invited him up into his chariot.

"Let me finish my game and I will come on my own. I'll follow the track of the chariots," called the lad. So Conchobar went on his way and when he arrived at the smith's house he forgot to mention that his nephew would be following.

In order that the King and his party would not be disturbed the smith set a great fierce hound to guard the place. Not only did the hound have the strength of a hundred ordinary dogs but it obeyed no one except its master, Culain. It would take a turn through the entire district and then lie guarding the house so that none dared approach—so fierce, so cruel and so savage was the watch-dog.

When Setanta came to the lawn in front of the smith's house the hound stood bristling before him. It threw back its great head and barked so loudly that the echo could be heard through the length and breadth of Ulster. Then it leapt forward, ready to fling its full fury at the invader.

Setanta, who had been up to his old trick of hurling his ball and chasing it, now hurled it straight at his enemy—and with such force and accuracy that the ball hit the monster in the mouth, plunged its way down its throat and through his body. Then the boy took hold of the hound and dashed it to its death against a rock.

The savage barking had brought Conchobar, Culain and the chiefs out of the house. They all watched in fascination and horror as the little fellow held up the carcass of the dog. One of the chiefs ran quickly and lifted the boy on to his shoulders and carried him to the King and his host.

But when Culain realised that his guard hound was dead he was angry. "There's little welcome for you here, boy, for without my dog how can I protect my flocks and my herds and the land that is my livelihood?"

"Don't be worried on that account," quickly retorted Setanta. "I shall see to it that you lose nothing. Give me a pup of the same breed and I will rear it myself, but until it is old enough and big enough to become your watch-dog I will guard your lands and protect your property."

Cathbad the Druid who was of the party heard these words and spoke up: "Well said, boy—and from now on your name will be Cuchulain, the Hound of Culain."

From that time on the boy was no longer known as Setanta, but Cuchulain.

Boy deeds of Cuchulain and the wooing of Emer

Some time after that Cuchulain overheard Cathbad speaking to the older boys, saying, "If any young man takes up arms today, his name shall be greater than any other name in Ireland, but his span of life will be short."

As Cuchulain valued fame above long life he went immediately to the King, his uncle, and persuaded him to allow him to take up arms—a recognition that he had attained manhood. Although Conchobar gave him a choice of weapons, naught but the King's own sword and shield along with two of his spears would satisfy the young warrior.

When Cathbad realised that Cuchulain was acting on his prophecy he commanded a chariot be brought to test Cuchulain's powers. When Cuchulain tried its strength, he broke it to pieces along with seventeen other chariots kept for the young nobles of Emain. Again it was only the King's own chariot that would satisfy the boy who had achieved manhood, and in it he set out for the border of Ulster to prove his status as a warrior.

When he came to the house of the three sons of Nechtar who were deadly enemies of the Ulstermen, he was challenged by each of the sons in turn, and each time he met the challenge. The first son Cuchulain killed by hurling an iron ball at his head; the second he pierced through the heart with a mighty thrust of his uncle's great spear, Venomous; and the third he wrestled in the ford of the river, overpowering him and striking off his head with Conchobar's sword. Then Cuchulain set fire to the house of the three brothers and carried off their heads in his chariot as a trophy.

On his way back to Emain he chased and caught two wild stags which he bound to the back of his chariot. Then he brought down a flock of white swans with a sling shot, being careful not to kill them, and tied them to the harness of his chariot.

So he returned to the palace not only a proven man but so aflame with his deeds and the blood-lust that was awakened in him that a shudder ran through those who stood on the look-out. The wildness left Cuchulain only when women ran naked from Emain to meet him, and he was overcome with shame.

From that time all the women of Emain, young and old, loved him for his handsome looks, the beauty of his body, his sweetness of speech, his bravery, his skill in sports and games and his great good sense. He excelled in games of chess and draughts as well as outdoor pursuits. Indeed his only shortcoming in the eyes of the women was his youth, for he was still smooth-faced and beardless. The men found him too beautiful and attractive to their womenfolk and altogether too daring. So the men persuaded Conchobar to send nine men into each of the provinces of Ireland to seek a wife for Cuchulain. Then the womenfolk, they felt, would be safe. Besides, he was the son of a god and destined to die young, if Cathbad's words were true, in which case he might leave no son and heir in his own likeness.

While the messengers looked for a suitable bride, Cuchulain himself decided to court Emer, the beautiful and talented daughter of Forgall Manach. In his eyes she was his only equal in age, appearance, breeding and skill—indeed the only girl in Ireland who would be, for him, a fitting wife.

Clothed in his white-hooded shirt embroidered with gold and his crimson five-folded tunic fastened with a gold brooch, Cuchulain mounted his chariot and drove to where Emer and her foster-sisters sat on the green lawn in front of Forgall's stronghold. Not wanting to embarrass the girl in front of her sisters Cuchulain addressed her in the secret language of poets. As he spoke to her in riddles she, being his equal in all things, replied also in riddles. Cuchulain, still speaking the language of poets, declared his love and asked why they should not be married. Emer in poet-speak declared her love for Cuchulain but warned him that no man could marry her before he had passed many tests of bravery and daring. Then Cuchulain returned to Emain.

When Forgall, who had magic powers, heard of Cuchulain's wooing of Emer he went in disguise to Emain and persuaded Conchobar to send Cuchulain to Scotland, where he could learn the finer points of war from a wild female warrior of that place. Before Cuchulain sailed for Scotland he secretly visited Emer, and the two swore to be true to each other.

So the young warrior set out on a journey to a wild country where he was to accomplish many a task and trial of cunning, bravery, strength and skill. With each challenge met he grew in stature and assurance. Little did he know that in his absence Forgall, who called Cuchulain "the wild one from Emain", promised Emer in marriage to Lugaid, a great king of Munster. But when Emer was brought to Lugaid she took his face in her hands and declared to him her love for Cuchulain. So Lugaid, for fear of Cuchulain and because he was an honourable man, sent her back to her father.

His achievements behind him, Cuchulain returned to Emain. As soon as he had told his story he set out to claim his bride in his scythe-chariot, for Forgall's stronghold was now fortified against his coming. Upon arriving, it was with his hero-leap that Cuchulain scaled the three walls of the fortress and landed inside the court. There he made three attacks, killing eight men in each attack. Only the three brothers of Emer escaped his onslaught. Forgall, while trying to escape from Cuchulain's wrath, leapt from the wall of the court and fell to his death.

The victorious Cuchulain gathered up Emer and her foster-sister and two sacks of gold and silver and set off for Emain. But Forgall's sister and her men followed in furious pursuit. At each ford of the river Cuchulain was attacked and each time he slew his attackers, so that the streams ran red with blood. Toward the fall of night Cuchulain and Emer came to Emain Macha.

There Cuchulain was given the headship of the young men of Ulster. He was chief among the warriors, poets, musicians, trumpeters and jesters. Of him the poet said. "He is as hard as steel and as bright, Cuchulain, the victorious son of Dechtire."

So it happened that after the long courting, the hardships, the great feats of endurance and the tests of skill and bravery, Cuchulain took Emer for his wife. Conchobar and the chief men of Ulster welcomed her warmly. And Conchobar led them to the House of the Red Branch which, with the Royal House and the Speckled House, made up the great chief palace of Ulster. In the House of the Red Branch were kept the heads and weapons of defeated foes. There Cuchulain took his place among the twelve chief heroes of the House. And Cuchulain and Emer lived happily together.

The Champion's Portion

There was at the court of King Conchobar a chief who delighted in stirring up trouble. His name was Bricriu and he was known as Bricriu of the Bitter Tongue. Bricriu had built himself a great house to the same plan as the House of the Red Branch in Emain. It was constructed of the finest materials in Ireland by the best craftsmen in the land. It included a drinking hall with a royal seat set with precious stones and wrought in gold and silver, and around it were the twelve seats of the twelve heroes of Ulster.

When the house was ready Bricriu invited Conchobar and all the chief men of Ulster to a great feast. In his heart he was determined to stir up strife between the chiefs if he could. But the men of Ulster knew Bricriu's wily ways and distrusted him, and so they agreed to accompany the King on the condition that Bricriu would leave the hall after he had received his guests and before the feasting began.

Bricriu agreed readily enough to the conditions laid down by the chiefs, but secretly he went first to a chief called Laegaire, then to Gonall and finally to Cuchulain. First he flattered each man telling him what a champion he was and how great his reputation was, but then he asked slyly of each, "What hinders you from gaining the championship of Ireland forever? If you could win the Champion's Portion at my house, would you not be recognised forever as the champion of all Ireland?" Then he offered a prize for the champion—a vat of wine big enough to hold three men, along with a prime seven-year-old boar and a prize seven-year-old bullock. "That is the Champion's Portion of my house," he said to each in turn, "and as you are a hero of Ulster it is but right that you should be given the Champion's Portion. So at the end of the day, when the feast is laid out, send your chariot-driver to claim it on your behalf." This was Bricriu's way of stirring up dissension.

Sure enough, when Conchobar and the chiefs arrived at his home and were ushered into the banquet hall Bricriu honoured his agreement and left the hall. As he was leaving for the watch-tower he turned and bade the musicians hush their playing and he called out: "The Champion's Portion of my house is worth the having. Let it be given to whoever you think is the greatest hero in Ulster."

As the servants began to distribute the food there was a stir and the chariot-drivers of Laegaire, Gonall and Cuchulain each went forward on their master's behalf. A quarrel broke out during which someone called out, "Give it to Cuchulain, he is the bravest of all." Then Laegaire and Gonall put on their shields and took hold of their swords and together attacked Cuchulain until Conchobar came between them and parted them.

"Put up your swords," he said. "This night the Champion's Portion shall be divided among the entire company and we shall leave it to be decided by Ailell, king of Connaught, at a later time."

So Bricriu's plan to foment trouble was foiled. But the quarrel between the three heroes was unresolved and it broke out once more when the three of them were back in Emain, so that Conchobar again had to step in. He bade the contestants go to Cruachan in Connaught to have their claims judged by King Ailell and Queen Maeve. "And if they can't settle the matter, go to Curoi in Munster. He is a wizard but fair-minded and wise in these matters."

Laegaire and Gonall, still quarrelling between themselves, yoked their chariots and set off for Cruachan but Cuchulain lagged behind amusing the women of Ulster with his tricks and juggling until his charioteer approached him saying, "You lazy man, have you lost your courage? The Champion's Portion will be lost to you forever if the men of Ulster reach Cruachan before you."

"I never thought of that; but there is still time. Yoke the chariot for me at once."

Then began a race that could be heard across Ireland. The thunder of horses' hooves shook the earth of Cruachan so that weapons fell from the racks and strongholds began to shake. The noise of the advancing chariots reached the ears of Maeve and she wondered greatly at thunder on such a clear day until her daughter, looking from the window, called out, "I see chariots coming!"

"Who comes in the first?" asked the Queen.

"A fine chariot indeed of newly polished wicker-work; it has two black wheels and it is drawn by two evenly matched dappled greys. In the chariot is a big stout man with a long forked beard. He is dressed in purple and ornamented with gold. His shield is bronze, edged with gold, and he has a javelin in his hand."

"I know him well," replied the mother. "He is mighty Laegaire of the Red Hand, a storm of war and a knife of victory. His sword cuts through men like a knife slices leeks. He'll slay us all unless he comes in peace!"

"But Mother, now I see another chariot," called the princess. "It is just as fine as the first and in it is a fair man, with long waving hair; his face is red and white, he is wearing a clear white vest, a blue and crimson cloak and his shield is brown, with yellow bosses and a bronze edge."

"I know that one too," said Maeve. "He is a growling lion and a living flame, valiant Gonall the Victorious. He will cut us up like trout upon a stone unless he comes in peace."

"But Mother, now I see yet another chariot," called the princess, "and this one is of fine wood and wicker-work, it has iron wheels and a curved yoke with gold over-lay. I see in the chariot the most handsome man in Ireland, yet he looks dark and sad. He is wearing a crimson tunic with a gold brooch, a long white linen cloak and a white hood embroidered with gold. His hair is black and his looks would melt your heart. His glance is like a flame of firelight and the light of heroes shines around him."

"I know well who that one is," said Maeve. "He is more to be feared than the others. His voice raised in anger is like the crashing of a stormy ocean, his wrath is deadly. We shall be ground like fresh malt in a mill if this Cuchulain comes in anger." Then the Queen turned to her daughter, "Tell me, are there more chariots?"

"The men of Ulster follow in chariots so numerous that their horses' hooves sound like thunder on the roof, and their trampling shakes the earth beneath them."

Maeve was now truly frightened but she gave orders that the men of Ulster be cordially welcomed. And so it was. When the heroes and men of Ulster arrived at the stronghold of Cruachan they were given a warrior's reception and were feasted for three days and nights.

After three days Ailell asked their business. Conchobar explained about the feast and the dispute over the Champion's Portion and the decision to ask Ailell for a settlement. This made Ailell angry. "It is no friend who does this to me, for I shall surely arouse the hatred of two heroes if I make a decision. I must have time to think this thing through — three days and three nights."

So the men returned to Ulster leaving the three contestants at Cruachan. That night Ailell put the heroes to a test.

They were given a room to themselves and a feast was served. After nightfall three magic beasts in the shape of monstrous cats were let out from the cave of the fairy people of Cruachan, and they stole into the room where the heroes were feasting.

At the sight of these creatures Laegaire and Gonall clambered up into the rafters and stayed there until morning, but Cuchulain waited until one of them made to attack him. Then he drew his sword and struck the monster. It showed no further sign of fight and Cuchulain kept guard all night until the beasts disappeared at daybreak.

When Ailell came in the next morning he laughed at Laegaire and Gonall up in the rafters and said, "Aren't you now content to yield the championship to Cuchulain?"

"Indeed we are not," replied the heroes. "We fight men, not beasts."

So Ailell sent the three contestants to spend a night with his father Ercol, who devised yet another test: the heroes, in turn, were to go by night to fight the witches of the valley.

Laegaire was first to go but the witches beat him soundly, taking his arms and armour. Gonall, too, was beaten and they took his spear, but he brought his sword back with honour.

Then Cuchulain made his way to the valley where the witches screamed and attacked with such vehemence that his spear was splintered, his shield broken and his clothing ripped away. But a great anger fell upon Cuchulain who turned on the witches, cutting and gashing them until the valley ran with blood. Carrying their battle cloaks he returned to the house. But still Laegaire and Gonall refused to acknowledge Cuchulain as the champion.

The following day Ercol himself fought with each of the heroes in turn. He had no trouble defeating Laegaire and Gonall, but he was no match for Cuchulain who not only beat him but tied him to the wheels of his chariot and took him back to Cruachan. Still the other two heroes would not admit defeat.

Ailell was now most upset, but Maeve said that she had a plan. First she called in Laegaire and said to him, "It is only right for you to have the Champion's Portion. Here is a bronze cup with a bird embossed in silver on the bottom. Don't let anyone see it but take it back to Emain, then show the cup and claim your right."

Next she called in Gonall and gave him a silver cup with a bird embossed in gold on the bottom and told him to do the same.

Then she called in Cuchulain who was playing chess and who at first refused to go. But when he did she gave him a gold cup with a bird designed in precious stones on the bottom and sent him on his way.

So the heroes, each secretly well pleased, said farewell and drove back to Ulster where a banquet was prepared. When the Champion's Portion was set aside Laegaire rose to claim it, producing his bronze cup as proof of his worth. Quickly Gonall rose up and produced his silver cup as proof of his worth. "See the difference in our cups," he said, "so it is to me the Champion's Portion belongs."

When Cuchulain produced his cup of red gold with its bird of precious stones, the King and the chief men agreed that he indeed was the champion. It was then that Laegaire and Gonall claimed that Cuchulain had bribed Queen Maeve; the quarrelling broke out again and Conchobar had to come between them.

"You will have to go to Curoi of Munster who is a wizard, wise and just, and he will use enchantments to find the best hero," decreed Conchobar.

So the following day the three disputing heroes went to where Curoi lived in a magic fortress. The wizard was away from home planning enchantments to test the contenders, for he knew they were coming, but the heroes were made welcome by his wife. She told them that they would have to take turns in guarding the stronghold at night, beginning with Laegaire who was the eldest.

It was a still, silent night and Laegaire was telling himself that he would have a quiet watch when he spied a brooding shadow emerge from the sea. This shadow then took on the form of a huge giant that reached the sky. His spears were stripped oak trees which he hurled at Laegaire who at first dodged them. But the giant grabbed Laegaire, lifted him up and squeezed him half to death before throwing him over the magic wall of the fortress into a mud heap.

The next night Gonall went out to keep watch, but that hero fared no better than Laegaire.

On the third night Cuchulain himself went to the watch-tower. It was at midnight that the sounds rang out, and in the cold light of the moon nine grey shapes moved across the marsh. Undaunted by Cuchulain's challenge they shouted at him and advanced. So Cuchulain sprang forward and hacked them down each one, then nine more shapes as they loomed toward him, until three times nine lay in a dead heap.

As the night wore on an eerie sound floated up from the lake and a great, slimy worm oozed upwards with its gaping mouth pointed at the watchman on the tower. With one great leap Cuchulain grasped the loathsome head, strangled the repulsive creature and tore out its heart.

It was near daybreak that the enormous shadow shaped like a giant came at him westward from the sea. The shape stretched out its hand to grasp Cuchulain as it had Laegaire and Gonall, but Cuchulain leapt his salmon-leap at the head of the monster and brought the creature down with his sword. With that it vanished

and was seen no more.

Only then did Cuchulain realise that his fellows had indeed been flung over the wall of the fort for it was hugely made, both broad and high. Kindled by his anger he took himself a way back then ran, barely shaking the dew-tipped grass, and leapt fair across the middle of the wall and landed at the door of Curoi's house.

There Curoi's wife was waiting, for she knew all that had happened and she spoke up, "The Champion's Portion must go to Cuchulain for he is greatest among you."

But Laegaire and Gonall disputed still, claiming that Cuchulain had friends among the Sidhe, the god-people, and that they had helped him. Then Curoi's wife bade the three of them return to Emain where Curoi himself would bring his judgement. So they bade her farewell and returned to the Red Branch.

One evening a good while after this, when Conchobar and his chief men, except for Gonall and Cuchulain, were gathered in the House of the Red Branch, they spied a great, ugly, awkward lump of a fellow coming into the hall. He was clad only in cow hide and had a grey cloak around him. He had hungry yellow eyes and in his right hand was an axe weighing fifty cauldrons of molten lead, its blade so sharp that it would shave the hairs of your arm if the breeze blew them across its edge.

The stranger approached the group and spoke. "Uath is my name, and it's going through the whole world and Ireland I am, looking for a man that will make an agreement with me and keep his word."

"What would the agreement be?" asked chief Fergus.

"See this axe of mine?" spake the stranger. "The man into whose hand it is put is to cut off my head today and tomorrow I will cut off *his* head; that is the agreement. I've heard tell of you men of Ulster, of your courage, your greatness and your skill with weapons. Who among you will make this agreement with me? Conchobar and Fergus I put aside because of their royal position, but who else among you will dare?"

It was Laegaire who sprang out on to the floor of the hall and taunted, "Kneel down, dimwit, that I may cut off your head today so that you can cut off mine tomorrow."

"So be it," said Uath, and he put spells on the blade of the axe before he laid his head on the block.

Laegaire struck such a blow with the axe that the blade buried itself deep in the block beneath. The head rolled to the floor and blood streamed through the hall of the house. Then terror fell on the crowd as Uath rose up, gathered his head and his axe to his breast and walked from the hall, his neck streaming with blood.

When the stranger returned the next night to keep the agreement Laegaire was nowhere to be found, but Gonall, who had heard of the deed, sprang forward to make a new agreement with Uath.

As it was the previous night so it was on this night and when Uath returned the following night Gonall was nowhere to be found.

"So, where is your courage and your daring, you men of Ulster? Is there not one among you who is true to his word?" taunted the great, ugly stranger. "Where is that poor squinting fellow you call Cuchulain? Is his word better than the others?"

"I will keep my word even without an agreement," shouted Cuchulain as he sprang to the floor of the hall. He grasped the axe and with a blow severed Uath's head and flung it like a football high into the rafters of the hall so that the building rang and shook.

When day came the men of Ulster watched to see if Cuchulain would keep his word. The hero appeared, pale and downcast. To Conchobar he said, "Stay with me until the agreement is sealed, for I fear death is upon me, but I would sooner die than break my word."

At the close of day Uath appeared. "Where is Cuchulain?" he demanded.

"Here," the hero replied firmly.

"Your speech is dull tonight," jeered the stranger. "The fear of death is upon you. But however much you fear, you have not failed me."

Cuchulain stepped forward and placed his head on the block. "Keep me not in torment, but make a quick end to it. Last night I did not delay. Now you act in the same way." Then he stretched out his neck and Uath raised the axe high into the rafters and its swishing was like a tree falling on a storm-tossed night.

But when the axe came down it was with its blunt side and it was the floor that it struck and Cuchulain was not touched at all. Then it was that the chief men of Ulster and Conchobar the king saw that this was indeed no fool but Curoi himself who had come to try the heroes with his enchantments.

"Rise up Cuchulain," said Curoi. "Among all the heroes of Ireland there is none to compare with you in bravery, truth or honour. From this day on the championship of all the heroes of Ireland is yours. The Champion's Portion is yours and your wife shall be first among all the women of Ulster. Whoever tries to put himself above you from today will himself be in mortal danger. I myself swear it." With these words Curoi quit the hall of the Red Branch and that was the end of the quarrel among the heroes for the Champion's Portion.

Great were the exploits of Cuchulain, who had many friends but also many enemies. Chief among his enemies was Queen Maeve of Connaught, who in time gathered to herself an army of all who hated or envied Cuchulain. Then she cast spells upon Cuchulain so that he imagined that the enemies of Ulster were ravaging his land. So he made war upon them.

On the eve of battle against the men of Ireland Cuchulain visited his mother Dechtire to bid her farewell. As she always did when her son called, Dechtire took a goblet of wine to him. But when Cuchulain took the vessel it was red with blood and not wine. Three times Dechtire filled the goblet and three times it was filled with blood. Then Cuchulain knew that his luck had left him and that he would not return alive from this battle. But he would not draw back, even though Dechtire pleaded with him.

So he went on his way with Cathbad, the Druid, and presently they came to a ford where a thin, white-skinned, golden-haired girl was washing, re-washing and wringing out clothing that was crimson with blood. And all the time the girl was keening and crying.

"Little Hound," said Cathbad to Cuchulain, "cannot you see that they are your blood-soaked clothes she is washing. Turn back before it is too late."

But Cuchulain would not draw back. Instead he sent Cathbad to Emain, carrying greetings to Conchobar and Emer from one who would never return.

Cuchulain continued his way alone and met three hags, each blind in the left eye. The women were cooking, beneath a rowan tree, a venomous hound in a cauldron into which they cast spells. One of the hags gave Cuchulain the shoulder-blade of the dog with her left hand and he took it in his left hand and ate it and then put it down on his left thigh. And the strength went out of his left hand and his left thigh, and Cuchulain knew for certain that his end was approaching.

As he arrived on the Plain of Muirthemne Cuchulain, riding his chariot, met the men of Ireland. Even though the strength was out of him, great was the slaughter committed by Cuchulain so that, to this day, the plain is red with the blood that was spilled. When his chariot-driver was speared Cuchulain was both driver and fighter and could still thrust so mightily with his spear that it went through the heads of the nine men behind his victim.

But Lugaird, son of Curoi, got the spear that had gone through so many heads, saying, "A king shall fall by this spear." And the first king to fall was the Grey of Macha—the king of the horses of Ulster, Cuchulain's own mount—wounded but not killed. Then Lugaird threw the spear again and this time it thrust through Cuchulain's body so that his blood spilled out, and he knew that this was his death-wound.

Gathering his entrails into his body he asked leave of his victors to drink from the lake beyond. He went down to the lake, drank a little and washed himself. West of the lake he spied a pillar of stone. With his breast-belt Cuchulain tied himself to the pillar so that he would not die lying down. His enemies gathered around him, wary even now of the hero of Ulster; and the Grey of Macha came back to defend Cuchulain as long as there was life in him. He killed fifty men with his teeth and thirty with each of his hooves.

Above Cuchulain's head shone the halo of the hero-light and a bird settled on his shoulder.

Then Lugaird lifted Cuchulain's hair from his shoulders and struck off his head while the men of Ireland gave three hearty shouts. As they did so the sword dropped from Cuchulain's hand and as it fell it struck off Lugaird's right hand so that it also fell to the ground. Then his enemies cut off Cuchulain's right hand and the hero-light faded, and left his head pale and bloodless.

When Gonall, who with the army of Ulster had gathered to attack its enemies, the men of Ireland, met the Grey of Macha dripping with blood he knew that Cuchulain was dead and went looking for his body. The man and the horse came to the body tied to the pillar-stone, and the Grey of Macha laid his head on Cuchulain's breast. "That body carries a heavy load of care for the Grey and for us all," said Gonall. He then went in search of Lugaird and when he found him, the two fought unto Lugaird's death; and Gonall took Cuchulain's head back to the pillar where his body was tied. Then he delivered Cuchulain's head and body to Emer.

Emer took the head of Cuchulain in her hands, washed it and wrapped it in a silken cloth, then clutched it to her bosom and began to cry and moan. For a long time she poured out all the love and sorrow in her heart and the old men and women of Ulster cried in pity and sorrow while the young men keened with harsh cries the loss of the champion, the Little Hound of Ulster.

Then a raging madness came upon Gonall and he set out in his chariot to bring vengeance upon the men of Ireland, as he had done to Lugaird. When Gonall returned with the heads of the men of Ireland Emer bade him lay them out on the green lawn, and he named them for her.

After that Emer told Gonall to dig a wide and very deep grave for Cuchulain; and she laid herself down beside her beloved husband and companion, put her mouth to his mouth and bade him farewell. "You who have been the love of my life, my sweetheart and lover, my only choice of all the men on earth, many are the women, wed or unwed, who have envied me your love until this day. Now I can no longer live without you."

So the life departed from Emer, and Gonall buried them in the one grave but raised only a single stone above them. And all the men of Ulster keened their passing.

Medieval France and Spain

In Roland and El Cid, France and Spain created national heroes who, like King Arthur, represent the ideals of medieval chivalry, loyalty, bravery and prowess in battle.

Perhaps France's greatest national hero is Charlemagne, who was actually Charles I, king of the Franks and Holy Roman Emperor. Unlike Arthur he is an historical figure and factual records of his life exist, even though some of the details have become legendary. The cycle of legends about Charlemagne is called the Carolingian Cycle from the Latin name *Carolus* because Charlemagne was not really French, but a Frank who spoke a Germanic language.

The Franks were a federation of Germanic tribes who, in the fifth century A.D., conquered most of what today we call Germany and France. In 771, when Charlemagne became king, he seized his brother's territories so that his kingdom also included what we today know as Switzerland, Belgium and most of Holland. During the forty-six years of his reign Charlemagne fought fifty-three campaigns to protect, safeguard and even increase his territories. Much of northern Spain and Italy were brought under tribute to him.

On Christmas Day in the year 800 he was crowned in Rome by Pope Leo III as emperor of the West and ruler of the Holy Roman Empire. His worst enemies were the Saxons from the north, but he also fought against Slavic tribes living in what is now East Germany and the Mohammedan rulers of Spain. When Charlemagne occupied the region in Spain between the Ebro River and the Pyrenees he was attacked and forced to retreat in haste. In the valley of Roncesvalles his rearguard, commanded by Count Roland, was annihilated. This is as much as history records of Roland who has become a true legendary hero. Details of the battle were recorded in 830.

Two hundred years later Europe was menaced by the Saracens who were Moslems and who were becoming a serious 'threat to Christianity. There were expeditions against the Mohammedan Moors in Spain and in 1095 Pope Urban II preached a fiery sermon which brought about the First Crusade, seen as a holy war.

Although Charlemagne had died in 814 legends had already gathered about his name. During the twelfth and thirteenth centuries many French *chansons de gestes*, or "songs of deeds", were composed about Charlemagne and other heroes, especially Roland. These poems were chanted by wandering *jongleurs* or minstrels during the Middle Ages. In them Charlemagne was presented as having spent his life fighting the Saracens and fact was often exaggerated into fiction. Religion was very important. So Roland became a great Christian hero in France just as El Cid did in Spain. Both heroes are characterised as champions of Christianity against infidels.

El Cid is represented as a champion of the Christian faith and, in his homeland Spain, it has been suggested that he be made into a saint because of his virtuous life.

Roland, Hero of France

Although the French epic *Chanson de Roland* has a factual basis, the hero, Roland, was probably a nobleman from Brittany. It is through legend that he has been given royal status, becoming even the nephew of Emperor Charlemagne the Great, head of the Holy Roman Empire, whose great deeds on behalf of France and the Catholic church made him famous in history.

His "nephew" and vassal, Roland, became the representative French hero of the early days of feudalism and chivalry—a hero who, according to the saga, could only be overcome by the treachery of one of the Franks themselves. So the traitor Ganelon who betrayed Roland becomes a Judas figure. In actuality the battle of Roncesvalles in which Roland was killed was not fought against the Moors or Saracens at all, but against the ancestors of what are the modern-day Basques.

So heroic became the proportions of the Roland story that both Spain and Italy took over elements from it. In Spanish versions a national hero, Bernardo del Carpio, defeats Roland in single combat. The chivalrous knight Orlando Furioso is an Italian version of Roland.

Like the epic of Gilgamesh the story of Roland is a tribute to friendship; as with Gilgamesh and Enkidu, David and Jonathan, the names of Roland and Oliver are forever joined in the telling.

And as with so many heroes, Roland's downfall is due at least partly to his pride.

Roland and Oliver become friends

The story is told that in the days when the Emperor Charlemagne, also known as Charles the Great, ruled both France and Germany he once called together the worthiest of his knights and barons so that they might renew their homage and he might reward them for their service in war. Among them was a count called Gerard who, through pride, and because the Emperor did not reward him as he had expected, rebelled against his lord and shut himself up in his stronghold at Vienne, to which Charlemagne laid seige.

For many months the stronghold was belaboured, but whenever the Emperor's warriors attempted to assault the walls Gerard's men drove them back with a shower of arrows from their crossbows. If any from within the fortress ventured through the gates and across the moat, they were turned back by the pointed lance of a swift, observant horseman. Both sides grew weary from waiting as they waged a war of nerves.

Among those within the stronghold were Gerard's nephew, Oliver, the most handsome and daring of his warriors, and Oliver's sister, Alda, who was just as comely and equally as brave as her brother. Among the forces of Charlemagne were the greatest champions of France and also the Emperor's young nephew, Roland, only recently knighted and anxious to prove himself in battle.

It is said that at times Alda put on armour and herself led a skirmish against the besieging army and that it was her custom to cheer on her uncle's men from the ramparts of Vienne. One day as she stood looking out across the devastated countryside a knight rode into view and approached close to the castle wall. To her eyes he appeared both manly and fair. The youth looking up beheld a warrior-maiden of such strength and loveliness that his heart leapt within him and, calling out, he asked her name. "Alda, and I am Count Gerard's niece," she replied.

"And I am Roland, nephew of Charlemagne. Even though we be enemies my heart flies up to you in love. Remember me, my lady, for we shall meet again."

As inactive months dragged by the young knights from both sides grew impatient with the skirmishes of a fruitless war and from having no real quest. Oliver, in particular, grew restive with the restricted life of the beleagured. One day, when Charlemagne's young knights were passing the slow days in camp by tilting among themselves, Oliver managed to escape the castle unnoticed. He was soberly dressed and carried plain arms so that none would recognise him. When he approached the young men and asked if he could join their sport, they welcomed him graciously enough.

Not even Roland proved a match for the stranger. His skill with both lance and sword drew not only admiration but curiosity, so that the knight had to break quickly away from their staying hands, leap on to his horse and make the castle gate.

It was Roland who led the chase and closed in on the youth as he approached the walls of the city. As he was drawing his sword ready to strike, he heard a cry from the ramparts and, looking up, he met the angry eyes of Alda. "Do not harm so worthy a foe. It is my brother Oliver whom you would slay."

Roland withdrew his hand instantly. "I shall let him go, for his own sake as well as yours." And Oliver rode through the gates unharmed.

From then on both Roland and Oliver longed for an end to the siege and for peace between their uncles; but both Charlemagne and Gerard were determined to emerge victorious from the war.

Then as Easter drew near a party of strange knights rode into Charlemagne's camp bringing tidings that the pagan king of Spain with an army of Saracens, bearing fire and the sword, had entered France. The Emperor's army was needed at once to drive them back.

Even then Charlemagne was loath to withdraw lest his honour be in question, because he had sworn to drive Gerard to his knees. Only when one of his counts put forward a plan did he listen, and the plan was this: that two knights be chosen, one from each camp, to meet in single combat and settle forever the quarrel between the Emperor and the Count. Charlemagne was highly pleased to have the possibility of withdrawing in honour, and immediately dispatched a messenger bearing a truce-flag to the gates of Vienne. There the knights of Count Gerard were as pleased as those of the Emperor to see the possibility of an end to a long and fruitless encounter.

Lots were drawn in both camps and it seemed a good omen when Charlemagne's nephew, Roland, was allotted the responsibility of upholding the name of the Emperor, for surely none was as brave or as eager to prove himself in service as he.

A day was appointed when the two combatants were to meet on an island meadow in the river Rhone which flowed between the fortress and the camp. On that day Roland, carrying a thick, wide shield provided by the Emperor, and his good sword Durendal whose blade was said to be proof against any attack, was ferried across to the isle. His opponent, known only as the Knight of the Red Plume, wore a helmet and armour said to be proof against the thrust of even the best-tempered sword.

On either bank of the river were gathered the knights and their followers from both armies. Among those of Gerard could be seen the lovely face and gracious figure of Oliver's sister, Alda, who paled when she recognised Roland as the Emperor's champion, for the Knight of the Red Plume was her brother. The combat was between Roland and Oliver, who instantly recognised one another as they saluted courteously before the battle began.

Never had odds been so evenly matched. In skill and courage the opponents were equally paired. More than two hours passed while they thrust and parried, giving blow for blow. Lesser knights would have fallen early in the battle. Their shields were dented and their armour badly bruised. At last the red-plumed knight was disarmed and brought to his knees by a mighty blow from Roland's sword Durendal, but the knight struggled to his feet and prepared to fight with his fists—to die rather than surrender.

At that Roland flung down his sword, scorning to fight an unarmed opponent. "Choose yourself another sword and a shield, then let us continue." So saying Roland rested while Oliver's attendants brought another sword from the castle—a blade called Hautclear, fashioned by a wonderful Jewish armourer.

Again the fierce fight waged until the hour of noon when Oliver thrust with such force that Hautclear snapped off at the hilt at the same time as Roland's Durendal became hopelessly buried in Oliver's shield. Both knights were without weapons, but neither was beaten. They each tore saplings from the earth and used them as bows until both were shredded into splinters. At last the two drew back and looked at one another.

"Pray let me rest awhile," breathed Roland. "I fear a fever for I have a great weakness upon me."

"So be it," responded Oliver, and courteously he not only stepped back but fetched water from the river to cool his adversary, determined not to take an unfair advantage of a sick man.

The sickness was a ruse on Roland's part to test Oliver's integrity; but as the Emperor saw his nephew being tended by the enemy he groaned, believing that his honour was lost, while Alda's heart stirred equally for her brother and for Charlemagne's nephew. Even as they watched, Roland sprang up and admitted that he was but testing Oliver, and the two men looked into each other's eyes and respect deepened into brotherly love . . . the love of comrades in arms who trust and respect each other.

"If we survive this trial will you allow me to wed your sister, if she will have me?" breathed Roland. "Then we shall truly be brothers."

"Indeed I shall. We shall be friends and brothers while ever we live," responded Oliver.

Till the going down of the sun the two challenged each other, and when swords proved useless and darkness fell, they wrestled like tigers until each could barely see the other for the sweat that poured from their brows. At last, as though with one mind, they lay still, looking hard at one another through the blackness. "It is God's will that we be equals as friends and brothers. Let us struggle no longer," they said. Quickly they embraced, holding each other close in friendship. "And never more shall we fight, except together against a common enemy."

So from that day on there was always to be a Roland for an Oliver, adventuring together, and fighting side by side against the Saracens, until their deeds were famous through France and beyond.

But before that, each had to persuade his uncle to accept the combat they had waged as satisfaction for the quarrel between the Emperor and the Count. So with honour restored, Charlemagne withdrew to fight the Saracens; and as the month of May brought new life to the stricken countryside around Vienne, Oliver gave his sister's hand to Roland and they were betrothed.

From then on Roland and Oliver were indeed brothers-in-arms until the great battle for which their names will be forever remembered.

The battle of Roncesvalles

For seven years the Emperor Charlemagne fought the Saracens in Spain. He conquered the enemy from coast to coast until only Zaragoza, set high in lofty mountains and ruled and defended by King Marsile, defied the power of the Emperor.

Now, Marsile, on the advice of his wily counsellors, sent messengers to Charlemagne at Cordova, bearing olive branches and gifts and a promise that if the Emperor would withdraw his army from Spain, Marsile would be baptised a Christian.

Charlemagne thought long about the offer then summoned his council, twelve heroes — chief among them being Roland, with his brother-at-arms Oliver, and including Archbishop Turpin and Roland's stepfather, Ganelon, who was secretly jealous of Roland and hated him. When Roland advised the Emperor not to trust Marsile, Ganelon opposed him, accusing Roland of pride in battle and declaring that a baptised Saracen was of greater glory to God than a dead one. So it was that Charlemagne chose Ganelon himself to go as envoy to Marsile and arrange the terms of peace.

It was an unhappy Ganelon who set out on the Emperor's mission and his displeasure deepened when he caught up with Marsile's chief messenger to Charlemagne who had delayed his departure so that the two envoys could travel together. The crafty Saracen drew Ganelon into a discussion about the hero, Roland. It was as though a dark cloud settled over Ganelon and soon he was accusing Roland of pride; in the manner of his speaking he let it be known how much he hated his stepson.

By the time they reached Zaragoza, Ganelon was boiling with rage against Roland and so became a victim of the cunning Saracens. Marsile and his envoy had little trouble in persuading Ganelon to turn traitor. Moreover he was to be paid in gold for his treachery. The plan was for Ganelon to return to Charlemagne and advise him that all was well and that the Emperor should return to France, leaving only a rearguard, headed by Roland, to cover the withdrawal. The rearguard would include Oliver and the Emperor's most gallant warriors who would be ambushed by the Saracens and slaughtered, every one of them. After such a loss the Emperor would never risk another campaign against the Saracens.

So it was that Charlemagne, mounted on his war-horse and with Ganelon at his side, headed a great army riding towards France, through the pass at Roncesvalles and in the direction of Gascony.

Roland and Oliver, with the good Archbishop Turpin and the mightiest warriors of France, were watching the dust of the army disappear in the distance when they heard a call of trumpets rumbling like thunder through the hills to the south! It was Oliver who climbed a rocky outcrop and saw the army of Saracens, one hundred thousand strong, heading for the pass at Roncesvalles. Only at the head of the pass did the army halt while the Moorish champions, twelve Saracen chiefs, vowed to slay Roland and the entire rearguard before pursuing the Emperor's army into France.

Although he could not hear their vows, Oliver had seen enough to understand. He descended the hilltop tower and ran, panting, to Roland. "Comrade!" he cried. "Blow your far-sounding war-horn, Olifant. Your uncle will hear it and know that we are betrayed, and he will return to aid us."

"God forbid it," replied Roland. "Should I ask help from my Emperor against these pagans? Own myself a coward? No—it is these unbelievers who shall perish. Have I not my good sword, Durendal, to aid me?"

Three times Oliver begged Roland to blow his magic horn. "See how small our troop is against the Saracen hordes!"

But Roland's pride forbade him. "Death I would choose, but not dishonour!"

Then Oliver knew that his prudence was in vain and that men would die that day. As though he too knew what was in store, Archbishop Turpin rode to the summit of a nearby hill and in ringing tones blessed the troops: "Should you die, it will be as martyrs, and your future home will be in Paradise forever."

Quickly Roland embraced his beloved Oliver. "I know now that Ganelon betrayed us; but fear not, Charlemagne will avenge us!"

"You would not blow your horn; Charles cannot help us. It is only left for us to fight!"

With the battle cry of Charlemagne "Montjoy! Montjoy!" upon their lips Roland's army spurred their horses against the advancing Saracen host. Great was the fray and deadly the combat. Each of the twelve champions did mighty deeds of arms. Roland himself cut down the nephew of King Marsile and Oliver slew the Saracen king's brother. One by one the twelve champions of Charlemagne brought down the twelve champions of King Marsile. The good priest, Turpin, struck a thousand blows crying out in the name of his Lord.

For all that, the weight of numbers eventually prevailed and great was the carnage among the Franks. Eventually, of the champions only Roland, Oliver and Turpin remained. It was then that Roland called to Oliver: "So many of our countrymen are slain. Our homeland will be devastated—and all because of treachery. Now I shall sound my horn of ivory, my Olifant, and Charlemagne will hear it in the passes and return with his army."

In amazement Oliver turned on his brother-friend. "Never will I approve it. To do so would be shameful! When I urged on behalf of our comrades who now lie dead you would not blow it. Would you now—to save yourself and me! Death I would choose, but not dishonour!"

When the Archbishop heard the two friends speaking sharply he interrupted: "Good knights, put by your anger. The horn will not save the lives of the gallant dead; us it will not save for the Emperor is too far away. But sound it now, good Roland, that your uncle may avenge our deaths and save our bodies from the wild beasts."

"You speak well," said Roland, and putting Olifant to his lips he blew with all his might. The echo carried the sound over thirty miles across mountains and through valleys to the Emperor's ears.

"That is Roland's horn I hear, our rearguard is attacked!"

"That cannot be," said Ganelon. "It is thunder in the hills."

A second time Roland lifted Olifant to his lips and blew with all his might.

"That is Roland's horn I hear, I'm sure. Our rearguard is attacked!"

But Ganelon laughed. "Perhaps he hunts the wild boar and is boasting as usual. Let us ride on, sire, to France."

A third time Roland lifted Olifant to his lips, and summoning up all his strength he blew a long blast.

Then the Emperor knew indeed that Roland was calling him. He looked hard at Ganelon, knowing in his heart what treachery had been worked; so Ganelon was put in chains. The trumpets sounded, and the valleys echoed with the sound of flying hooves as the Emperor and his army answered the call of Roland's horn.

Back at Roncesvalles Roland hung his horn once more around his neck and side by side he and Oliver rode back into the battle. Roland slew King Marsile's son, then, when the King attacked, cut off Marsile's right hand so that the Saracen king fled, mortally wounded, back to Zaragoza.

But great was the Frankish loss and Roland, Oliver and Turpin stood alone.

Emboldened by the sight, a Saracen nobleman rushed at Oliver and pierced him with his lance from behind. Dazed and blinded with his own outpoured blood Oliver called to Roland, and shouting "Montjoy! Montjoy!" he continued to strike out with his sword. Now he knew not friend from foe and coming upon Roland he struck out not recognising the face of his dearest friend, and clove his helmet but harmed not the head inside it.

Roland, mindful of their recent quarrel, asked gently, "Comrade and brother, was that blow meant to kill Roland who loves you so? To avenge a wrong?"

"Roland, I hear you but I see you not. Would I seek vengeance on my friend? There is nothing to avenge. It is for you to forgive the blow I struck you all unknowingly."

"I have no hurt," said Roland. "Pray God we meet again in Paradise."

And Oliver, the gentle and courteous noble knight, fell dead, his face to the east while Roland wept over his body. "Many days have we been comrades together. No ill you did me ever, nor I to you. Now you are dead and it is a pity that I live."

Now of all the Franks only Roland and Turpin were left, and Turpin was wounded. The Saracens speared both their horses and withdrew to join their King.

Roland, wounded and in great pain, with stumbling feet and unsteady hands, bound up Turpin's wounds then fetched one by one the bodies of the champions of France and laid them at Turpin's feet. Last of all was Oliver, his friend whom he loved as a brother, whose body he now lay on a broken shield. And Turpin blessed and absolved them all.

Only then, weak with pain, Roland himself fell into a swoon. Slowly and painfully the Archbishop lifted Olifant the ivory horn, from around Roland's neck and slowly the dying prelate staggered to the stream to fetch water so that Roland could be revived. But the good priest was weak unto death and he, too, fell forward and died with the horn in his hand.

When Roland awoke from his swoon he guessed what had happened, and crossing the Archbishop's hands over his breast he prayed God to receive his soul.

Now death was very close to Roland himself. Taking Olifant in one hand and his sword Durendal in the other he slowly crossed a field and climbed a little hill one bowshot within the realm of Spain. At the top of the hill he sat down; there, a Saracen who had been lying on the ground pretending to be dead, now crept up to steal his sword. But Roland saw him and with his ebbing strength struck out with his horn, slaying the man but shattering the horn.

Then as he lay there he looked at his sword, Durendal, and knew that he would never again use it. "Great deeds have I achieved with you, my trusty Durendal. Many lands have I conquered for my uncle. Must I leave you to these pagans?"

Three times the hero struck at a nearby rock with the sword, hoping to shatter the blade. But the steel only grated on the rock and Roland knew that his strength was spent and his life fading.

So placing Olifant, his shattered ivory horn, and Durendal, his own true sword, side by side Roland lay himself face down across them, with his face towards Spain so that Charlemagne and the Franks when they arrived would see that he died undefeated. After praying to his God for the forgiveness of all his sins Roland held his glove toward Heaven, and it is said that St. Gabriel himself received it, then bore his soul to Paradise.

Soon after Roland's spirit had departed, Charlemagne and his army came galloping out of the mountains into the valley of Roncesvalles where his entire rearguard lay dead. Terrible was the vengeance taken by the Emperor. He pursued the Saracens to the very walls of Zaragoza, slaying thousands. With Marsile dead of his wounds, the Emperor returned to Roncesvalles to bury his slain knights with reverence and honour.

Climbing himself to the summit of the hill where, on the blood-stained hillock, lay the body of his nephew, Charlemagne gathered Roland's form in his arms, lamenting loudy: "Never again shall fair France behold a knight so worthy! Who shall fight for me now that my nephew Roland is no more? Who will honour me now that Roland is dead? Would that I, too, should die and join my valiant kinsman in Paradise!" And Charlemagne, the Emperor, wept.

The fallen knights were buried with all honour in the field but the bodies of Roland, Oliver and Turpin were carried to Blaye and buried with ceremony in the great cathedral there. Then the Emperor returned to his palace at Aix where Alda the Fair, Oliver's sister and Roland's betrothed bride, waited the return of her loved ones.

"What news of Roland, my bridegroom-to-be?" she asked.

Tearing at his long white beard the Emperor turned away. "Speak no more, dear child. Roland is dead, but his soul is with God."

"Then God forbid that I should live without him," lamented Alda and fell dead at the Emperor's feet.

Ganelon, the traitor, was tried and sentenced to death, his name forever reviled; but the memory of Roland and Oliver is still an inspiration not only in France but wherever friendship and chivalry are held dear.

El Cid Campeador of Spain

The story of El Cid is Spain's greatest legend. His exploits were the subject of medieval manuscripts of the twelfth and thirteenth centuries in Latin, Hebrew, Arabic and Spanish. Modern Spanish scholars have authenticated the life of the hero, Rodrigo de Vivar. A play about El Cid written by the French dramatist Corneille was first performed in 1636.

In reality El Cid was an outlaw who had a mixed band of Christian and Moslem warriors. The name Cid was given him by the Moors and means "master". Campeador means "challenger" because at the beginning of a battle he would issue a challenge to single combat.

Certainly both Roland and El Cid were noble, full of great strength and bravery. They were fearless, agile, daring and intelligent. They possessed the qualities of great heroes.

A thousand years ago Spain was overrun by the ferocious Moors, a marauding Moslem tribe which crossed the Strait of Gibraltar from Africa to fight for their god Allah and "his one true prophet", Mohammed. After they seized and occupied most of Spain they fell to quarrelling among themselves. The Spaniards also fought among themselves as Spain was made up of rival kingdoms, so that the country was rent by constant skirmishes and frequent battles.

Among the Christian kings of Spain, Ferdinand I of Castile and Leon was the richest and the most formidable. It was one of his knights who became the legendary hero, El Cid.

171

Rodrigo becomes knight

Rodrigo was the best-loved son of Don Diego de Vivar, a wise and scholarly noble of the court of King Ferdinand of Castile. At seventeen he was not only good-looking but had muscles like tightly twisted cords; he was as strong as a young bull but as lithe and agile as a dancer. He loved nothing better than to ride the swiftest steed in his father's stable, to shoot the bow in local contests, and he excelled with both sword and lance. He was impatient to be known as a man and to win his knighthood.

His father, on the other hand, preferred to follow the paths of scholarship and learning in the library of his comfortable estate near Vivar — away from the gossip and intrigue of the court. Not only intrigue, but open quarrelling, even among the King's three sons. So violently and openly had they disputed of late over their share of their father's inheritance — dividing up in their minds the kingdom between them while the old man was still alive — that King Ferdinand had summoned his Council of State to help him settle once and for all the question of his succession and inheritance. Otherwise he feared civil war.

Don Diego had been summoned. Much against his will he would have to forsake his manuscripts, maps and books to attend the assembly. Rodrigo, when he heard the news, began to fret with impatience, begging his father to allow him to accompany him to court, if only as a body-guard and protector on the way.

"But Father, there could be Moorish bandits on the road. You need me to protect you," he insisted.

"Then you shall come; but not because I need your protection. Rather so that you will learn for yourself what humbug goes on at the court, how petty and tiresome it all is, and how much better off you are here at Vivar," the old noble answered.

So Rodrigo, wearing a new scarlet cape, sat behind his father on their ancient horse Pitiuso and set off for the royal capital of Burgos. Rodrigo's mind was full of knight errantry in which he had visions of himself brandishing a sword and leading an onslaught against the Moors whom he hated.

On the evening of the first day of their journey father and son put up for the night at a small inn just outside the city of Valladolid. In the courtyard of the inn there was a well which was the centre for gossip, and Rodrigo was drawn there by the stories the soldiers were telling of their fights with the Moslems. While he was sitting there drinking it all in he heard a voice in the distance calling desperately for help. Rodrigo tagged along with a party of soldiers who ran in the direction of the cries which were coming from the figure of a man buried up to his waist in quicksand, held fast and quickly sinking.

"For the love of God, won't someone help me?" cried the struggling man. "Get me out of this pit of death."

But not one of the soldiers made a move to help him. Instead they drew back in alarm and began to cover their faces and look away. For the man in the quicksand was ravaged with leprosy, his face disfigured and his hands but ghastly stumps of dying flesh.

Rodrigo felt no fear; only deep pity ran like fire through his heart, and without stopping to think he reached out and grasped the struggling leper with both hands, slowly and painfully withdrawing the abject and almost naked figure from the bog. The man was trembling all over and shivering with cold. Rodrigo quickly took off his new crimson cape and wrapped it around the leper, while the soldiers backed away in horror.

"Do not touch that which is unclean," called one.

"Do you want to become a leper yourself?" asked another.

"Let him be and look after yourself," added the third.

But Rodrigo's heart filled with compassion. He knew that there would be no room at the inn for a leper, so he led the man to the stables where his horse Pitiuso was being fed. There he fixed a bed of clean straw and settled the leper, still wrapped in his cape, as comfortably as he could. "The fellow will be hungry," he thought, so he left him and went to fetch food and wine which he knew he would have to smuggle out of the inn. Secretly he put aside his own share of the evening meal, and as soon as his father was asleep he crept out to the stables with his offering.

As he approached he heard Pitiuso neigh softly, yet when he got there the stranger had disappeared. The straw was still warm and he could see the shape where the man had huddled. Moreover the crimson of his cape, which was neatly folded, caught his eye.

He started forward, and was arrested by a soft voice behind him calling, "Whom do you seek?" Whirling around he was startled to see an apparition. A tall figure, clad only in a pure white tunic from which shone a heavenly light, was standing with arms raised in the doorway of the stable.

"Who are you? What do you want of me?" demanded Rodrigo.

"I am Lazarus, come back from the dead. Do not be afraid. Today you stretched out to me a helping hand. You fearlessly risked your life to save mine. God will reward you. I come with the promise that from this day forward you will be unconquerable. You will do great deeds and become known throughout the land; you will die honourably; and your name will be remembered forever." With these words the vision smiled and made the sign of the cross, then vanished from Rodrigo's sight.

Slowly the young man gathered up his cape and returned to his bedchamber in the inn, resolved never to tell any man what had happened that night.

For two more days father and son journeyed towards the capital—long, hot, dusty days with never a bandit in sight, only the glare from the sun on the boulders by the roadside. On the afternoon of the third day the travellers were parched with thirst and were weary.

Just where the road ran around the base of a stony hillside Pitiuso stopped suddenly, his head thrown back and ears alert. Rodrigo scrambled down and ran, sword in hand, to the rear of a rocky outcrop ready for any lurking bandit. There was not a soul in sight. But out of the shadows, picking its way over the rubble, came a sorry, disreputable-looking horse, its coat matted and lacklustre, its head sniffing constantly for edible grass or anything to help fill its empty belly. Rodrigo advanced and placed his arm around the neck of the pitiful creature which looked at him as though it were begging for friendship. He was obviously without an owner. Perhaps his master had been killed by bandits; who knows?

While the young man and the stallion were getting to know one another Don Diego rode over, smiling. "I'm not surprised he has no saddle. Only a fool would want that bag of bones," he said.

"Bag of bones he may be, but he has character, Father, and as he has obviously been abandoned I mean to have him for myself," said the young man.

"Then you are a fool," his father asserted.

"In that case I shall call him Babieca—fool—but I tell you he will give the lie to his name. Just wait and see!" Rodrigo jumped up on to the horse's bare back and sat there proudly. Babieca didn't even flinch, and when Don Diego rode off on Pitiuso they formed a procession—the old scholar sitting sedately in the saddle and the young man, riding bareback but upright, sharing something of his energy with his mount.

So they rode on. That night Rodrigo stabled the two horses at the inn and spent hours grooming Babieca who, after a feed enough for three horses and a good night in a comfortable stall, looked far less disreputable than he had the previous day. Rodrigo even invested in a second-hand saddle which he polished as carefully as he brushed Babieca. So father and son arrived at the capital in style.

On the day appointed for the Council of State, Rodrigo walked with his father down the long length of the Hall of Justice in the King's palace. They made their way through a throng of knights and nobles who were all brilliantly clothed, their brightly decorated capes and plumed helmets filling the great hall with bursts of colour. Even the walls were alive with pennants and banners intricately wrought in flashing hues of red, green, blue and gold. At the far end of the hall the King sat enthroned on a golden pedestal caressing his richly ornamented and bejewelled sword of state.

Amid this sea of colour Rodrigo's eyes were suddenly filled with a sight fairer by far than that of the courtiers or the ornamentation of the occasion. Standing by the side of a tall nobleman, whom Rodrigo recognised as the renowned Count of Lozano, was a girl whose beauty instantly smote his heart. Her long, dark hair shone like a raven's wing and her cheeks had the lustre of costly pearl.

Rodrigo, himself tanned from his journey, his own luxuriant hair shining like burnished copper, made an equally impressive sight. The gazes of the young man and the girl met at the same time. Both smiled involuntarily as though this were an instant of simultaneous recognition. The girl flushed slightly but didn't lower her eyes which followed Rodrigo as he advanced at his father's side.

But now he was catching at his father's arm and the girl saw them both look in her direction, and she knew that the old man was saying in reply to his son's question, "That is Jimena, the daughter of the Count of Lozano who guards her honour well and who, as yet, has always looked most unfavourably on any man who allows his eyes to rest too long on that pretty face."

While the old man spoke a trumpet blast rang down the length of the hall and the King rose to address the assembly. In due course it was the turn of Don Diego of Vivar to make his obeisance. Rodrigo, his son, knelt at his father's side before the King.

Legend has it that the King looked hard at the young man and said, "You have the stamp of a warrior and a champion. The time is soon coming when you will have the opportunity to prove yourself." Prophetic words spoken by a king.

That same afternoon Don Diego returned from the Council, which only the nobles attended, his face flushed and his habitual calm replaced with agitation and anger. To his son he poured out a story of insult and indignity. All had not gone well at the Council. While Don Diego advised the King to keep the kingdom intact, passing the succession to the eldest son, others argued for dividing the kingdom. The King was still undecided, but he had appointed Don Diego as tutor to the sons who were causing such a scandal at the Court. It was then that the Count of Lozano had spoken hotly, not only claiming that Don Diego was fit only to train the princes in witlessness and cowardice, but striking the old man across the face—an involuntary gesture caused by anger at not having been appointed tutor himself.

Rodrigo didn't hesitate. He immediately stretched out his hand for his father's sword, Tizone, which the old man unbuckled and handed silently to his son, his snow-white head bowed in hurt and shame. The youth strode quickly to the stable, saddled Babieca and rode straight to the castle of Belares where he knew he would find the Count. As he galloped along the road the vision of Jimena came to him, blotting out his father's shame. But only for an instant. The hot blood of anger would not cool so quickly, and he rode furiously into the castle courtyard arriving even before the Count had dismounted from his own horse.

Rodrigo challenged the Count with a rush of angry words. "I would not call him 'sir', who has so insulted my father. I have come to right that wrong. Draw your sword and let us fight!"

"Fight with you! A boy, who is not yet knighted? Go away and hold your peace," called the Count.

"Then it is you who is the coward," taunted Rodrigo. "Let it be told throughout the kingdom of Castile that the Count of Lozano is a liar and a coward."

Rodrigo's words were like a red cape to a bull. The Count, enraged, drew his sword and rode to the attack. The fight was on. Once as he swung forward the young man saw Jimena's face drift across his line of vision. The face was pale now, her eyes startled, her lips pressed tight together. For an instant the youth faltered, then thrust in under the Count's defence. Clearly his youth and vigour and his training at home were no match for a count who ate too much and drank too much and spent most of his time involved in the intrigues of the Court.

Rodrigo knew that he had his opponent at his mercy. "Apologise to my father and we will call it a fair fight," he called.

"Never! Cowardly son of a cowardly father. Fight on!" The Count lunged with his sword, but Rodrigo rose high in Babieca's saddle and with his father's sword, Tizone, smote the Count on the shoulder so that he was forced to drop his shield. A second blow clave the Count's helmet and his head in two. The Count of Lozano was dead.

The King's guard who had seen everything that happened lost no time in dragging Rodrigo, still panting from the battle, to the royal palace and into the great Hall of Justice. Other guards had been dispatched to summon Don Diego. Once again, father and son were in the presence of the King.

But before the King could speak Rodrigo had held out Tizone to his father, "I return your sword with your honour, sir. You are avenged and I will pay whatever penalty the King requires."

"Nay. Keep the sword, my son. It is now yours by right and deed. May you never know dishonour." So spoke the old man. As Don Diego finished, the King spoke up. His face was grim but his eyes smiled. "So you are a warrior and a champion, even as I said. Would you be a knight?"

"Indeed, sire, as my soul lives. You know I do."

"Then kneel before me." And the King touched the boy on the right shoulder with his own sword of state. "I dub thee Knight of Castile, by God and Santiago. Rise and be loyal in my service!" When Rodrigo stood before him the King held him at arm's length by the shoulders. "You are now a knight, but a young and impetuous one who has just killed a count, albeit in the course of justice. There is a penalty to pay for that. I hereby banish you from my presence and from my kingdom. You will be a knight with an errand far from home."

The newly knighted youth looked his monarch straight in the eye. "That I accept, my lord. Let my errand be to fight the Moors who batter at the boundaries of your kingdom. I vow to bring honour to Castile."

So it was that Rodrigo, knighted by the King and with his father's sword and his blessing, rode out on his steed Babieca to do battle against the mighty Moors. With him he carried the memory of the maiden, Dona Jimena, her beautiful face marked by pain and hurt, caused by the man who had killed her father.

Rodrigo becomes El Cid Campeador

Before Rodrigo de Vivar left the realm of the King he returned home to bid farewell to his mother and to ask her blessing. Already news of what he had done and of his banishment had spread through the kingdom. He was not alone in his impatience to rid the territory of Spain of the obnoxious Moorish invaders, and before he set out for exile he was joined by a band of caballeros who were determined to follow wherever he might lead them in their fight against the enemy.

Soon the outlaw band was winning the reputation of being invincible. Their heroic feats were spoken of in every castle and town of Castile. Reports of Rodrigo's bravery and daring came constantly to the ears of the King, who followed with interest and admiration the exploits of his youngest knight.

It so happened that one day, when Rodrigo and his band were making a reconnaissance through the barren lands which bordered the Moorish emirate of Zaragoza, he came across a Moorish trading party which fell easy victim to his assault. The party was led by an ancient Moor who threw himself at the mercy of the young knight, confessing that he was heading an expedition carrying jewels of priceless value to the Emir of Zaragoza who would have his head if they were not delivered safely.

This news aroused the curiosity of Rodrigo and the greed of some of his men, who clamoured to be shown such treasure.

The old merchant, thereupon, very reluctantly approached one of the mules which appeared to be carrying a miniature mosque draped with expensive silk and brocade cloth. Even more reluctantly, but at the urging of Rodrigo himself, the Moor pulled aside the drapery. Inside the structure sat a beautiful Moorish girl, who was obviously terrified by what was happening.

"This is a treasure. But what is it doing out in the desert and where are you taking it?" enquired Rodrigo.

"My lord. This princess is the bride-to-be of the Emir of Zaragoza. We carry her dowry to the Emir himself. That is why my lord is in danger."

Rodrigo's men began to chuckle and rub their hands with glee. "A fine ransom price she will fetch," they said. "Away with her to headquarters."

But Rodrigo was thinking of Jimena, and his father had brought him up to be chivalrous and merciful when mercy was justified. Now he silenced his followers, asserting that he would never molest a bride, even a Moorish one. And he gave the party leave to continue on its way.

Just as the merchants and their men were mounting and preparing to ride away, a thunder of hooves was heard and another marauding party rode up brandishing weapons. These were not Moors but Castilian brigands who preyed upon passing travellers, Moors and Spaniards alike. The leader of the bandits was a huge fellow with a startlingly red beard and he rode up on a white, pure-bred Arabian stallion, calling out to Rodrigo as he approached. When Rodrigo explained what he was doing the bandit laughed and introduced himself as Gonzalvo.

"Perhaps you can afford to be generous. As for me, no infidel dog escapes. My men outnumber yours three to one so you have a choice. We can share the treasure or I'll have your head and those of your men and divide the booty among my men—and I'll have the princess for myself."

"Oh no you won't," spat out Rodrigo. "You'll have to kill me first. It is true that your band outnumbers mine, but you and I are the leaders and equal. Let us fight this one out alone—or are you a coward?"

This speech only caused Gonzalvo to roar with laughter. "You speak bravely, stripling, but we'll see if your sword is as good as your words." Then, "Come, I'm joking," he said as Rodrigo's hand went to his sword. "You are but a child, and I say, 'Be on your way!'"

Gonzalvo's laughter died on his lips as Rodrigo sprang forward and offered him the greatest insult a Spaniard knew. He tugged at the man's beard and pulled out two strands of the bright red hair.

"So—that much for your leader," Rodrigo called out to the bandit band.

But already Gonzalvo had struck with his sword and Rodrigo's Tizone fell into the dust. It was then that Rodrigo sprang and hauled Gonzalvo bodily from his saddle, sending his sword flying; and the two men faced each other in what became the most renowned wrestling match that Castile had ever known. For a long time the giant and the youth circled and closed in on one another, neither one gaining the advantage, and both without their swords. Then Rodrigo was able to retrieve his sword which he brandished, driving Gonzalvo before him. A groan went up from the bandit's followers and a cheer from Rodrigo's band. Gonzalvo spat at the youth who picked up the brigand's sword which was now at his feet and tossed it to his opponent.

"Now fight on equal terms again," he called. As he cried he charged at the giant and the battle continued, both men beginning to show signs of fatigue. Again, Rodrigo's training and his youth stood him in good stead. He was more nimble-footed than the older man and he danced as he thrust, until the bandit swung and sliced at nothing. It was then that Rodrigo delivered the death-blow and Gonzalvo lay at his feet, his red beard turned up in the sunlight.

The Moors, who had been following the combat as excitedly as Rodrigo's own men, burst into a loud cheer, calling "El mio Cid, Campeador!"—My lord, the Champion. From that day on Rodrigo became known throughout Spain and the Moorish emirates as El Cid; and that name lives on in legend.

Calling down blessings from Allah the merchants went on their way, and Rodrigo sent Gonzalvo's men also on their way although many chose to cast their lot with his and join his band.

Soon after this El Cid was chosen by the King to fight, single-handed, for Castile against the champion of Aragon. After his victory the King pardoned El Cid who returned to the court at Burgos and was forgiven by Jimena, whom he courted with chivalry.

But his challenges were not over. When Prince Sancho was made king of Castile he made Rodrigo commander-in-chief of his armies, and whenver the occasion called for it the commander fought many a battle single-handed. A further feud between the King sons caused El Cid to lose the title of commander-in-chief, but he now had Jimena as his wife and she gave him strength in the trials that were to follow.

After many battles against the Moors and after he had conquered vast territories, El Cid became king of Valencia. Always he carried Tizone and rode Babieca into battle.

At the end, and in his final battle, Babieca stumbled over a tent rope and El Cid was thrown, breaking his shoulder. He was now no longer young, and long years of campaigning had taken their toll. He fell into a delirious fever and even the love of Jimena and the skill of the best doctors in Spain failed to rally him. He died calling for a united Spain.

When news of El Cid's death reached the fanatical Emperor Yusuf in Africa he quickly organised a fresh army. They marched on Valencia and besieged the city, surrounding it with one hundred thousand Moslem warriors. It was Dona Jimena who gave the orders for the gates of Valencia to be opened wide.

The besieging army beat a tattoo of drums and prepared to charge, when out of the city gates rode a fearful sight. Babieca in battle array led an avenging charge, and on his back sat El Cid himself, with Tizone at his side. The sight struck terror into Yusuf and his cohorts who believed that the champion had come back from the dead to avenge his countrymen. They fled in terror before the terrible apparition. Little did they know that on Dona Jimena's orders her husband's embalmed body had been laced into the saddle of the worthy Babieca who was to become part of the legend, foretold by Lazarus, of the invincible El Cid Campeador.

Bibliography

Ancient Greece
Baumann, Hans. *Hero Legends of the World*. London: Dent, 1975.
Bullfinch's Mythology: The Age of Fable. New York: Doubleday, 1968.
Graves, Robert. *The Greek Myths*. London: Penguin, 1960.
Green, Roger Lancelyn. *Heroes of Greece and Troy Retold from the Ancient Authors*.
   London: Bodley Head, 1975.
Homer. *The Odyssey . . . translated by E. V. Rieu*. London: Penguin, 1971.
_____. *The Odyssey . . . translated into English prose*. London: Oxford, 1972.
Lister, Robin. *The Odyssey . . . retold by Robin Lister and illustrated by Alan Baker*.
   London: Kingfisher, 1987.

Sumeria and Babylon
The Epic of Gilgamesh: an English version with an introduction by N. K. Sanders.
   London: Penguin, 1980.

Old Scandinavia

Baldwin, James. *The Story of Siegfried.* New York: Scribner, 1959.

Crossley-Holland, Kevin. *The Faber Book of Northern Legends.* London: Faber, 1977.

Green, Roger Lancelyn. *Myths of the Norsemen.* London: Penguin, 1985.

Harrison, Michael. *The Curse of the Ring.* London: Oxford, 1987.

Hosford, Dorothy. *Sons of the Volsungs.* New York: Henry Holt, 1949.

Kalevala: The Land of Heroes Vol. 1–2. Translated by W. F. Kirby. London: Dent, 1970.

Synge, Ursula. *Kalevala: Heroic Tales from Finland.* London: Bodley Head, 1977.

Volsunga Saga: The Story of the Volsungs and Niblungs translated by William Morris. London: Collier-Macmillan, 1967.

The Old Testament

The Bible: Old Testament. Exodus, Deuteronomy, Judges.

Old England

Beowulf: A New Translation by David Wright. London: Penguin, 1957.

de Troyes, Chrétien. *Arthurian Romances.* London: Dent, 1983.

Early Irish Myths and Sagas translated by Jeffrey Gantz. London: Penguin, 1982.

Green, Roger Lancelyn. *King Arthur and His Knights of the Round Table.* London: Penguin, 1985.

Hadfield, Alice M. *King Arthur and the Round Table.* London: Dent, 1964.

Lady Gregory. *Cuchulain of Muirthemne arranged and put into English by Lady Gregory.* Gerrards Cross, Buckinghamshire: Colin Smythe, 1933.

Malory, Sir Thomas. *Le Morte d'Arthur.* London: Penguin, 1969.

Ross, Anne. *Druids, Gods and Heroes from Celtic Mythology.* London: Hodder & Stoughton, 1986.

Picard, Barbara Leonie. *Hero Tales from the British Isles.* London: Penguin, 1963.

Sutcliff, Rosemary. *Dragon Slayer: The Story of Beowulf.* London: Penguin, 1983.

Medieval France and Spain

De Vivanco, Maria Luisa Gefaell. *El Cid: Soldier and Hero.* London: Hamlyn, 1967.

Goldstone, Robert C. *The Legend of the Cid.* London: Ward, 1963.

The Song of Roland translated by Dorothy L. Sayers. London: Penguin, 1981.

Index